EXPERIMENT

IN SURVIVAL

To Carly,
Hope you enjoy
the book, save me
a place for next
year

George Sigler

Published by:
VERO TECHNICAL SUPPORT
155 31ST Ave. SW
Vero Beach, FL 32968

Copyright © 2001 by George Sigler
Library of Congress Control Number: 2001090409
ISBN: 0-9711100-0-X

First printing: May 2001

Printed in the United States of America

Contents

Photographic Sections

Dedication

I want to dedicate this book to the memory of Pat Royce, author of *Sailing Illustrated*. Pat was perhaps my best friend in the boating community, and we had many wonderful sails together. He was one of my best friends, and I will always remember Pat kindness and generosity. Happy Sailing, Pat.

Introduction

The expedition Charlie and I took crossing the Pacific in a rubber raft came as a result of thousands of lives being lost at sea. I wanted to create a survival kit that would give direction and a goal to the castaway. When I developed the SIG II survival kit there was not extensive satellite emergency radio coverage as there is today. The castaway could not count on someone saving his life. Even today with the good emergency radios we have, there are areas of the ocean that still have poor coverage, and radios do fail or run out of battery power. I still believe that a boater should consider the possibility that he might have to sail to safety if his boat should sink.

I did a great deal of research in developing the survival kit, and I have given hundreds of speeches about survival at sea. I wrote this book because sailors still expose themselves to the dangers of crossing the oceans in small boats. And some of those boats are going to have trouble and sink. The information in this book will no doubt help keep a castaway alive, as they will have a better understanding of what is happening to their bodies as they might drift in a life raft. This book might give one person the knowledge that might one day save his life if he becomes a castaway.

Since my trip across the ocean, I have read a number of books about castaways that could have used the information I gained from my research to help them. In many cases I realized that if I had written a book that knowledge might have helped save someone's life. Well here is the book. I hope no one ever has to use the knowledge, but now it is available. I hope you enjoy the story, but most of all I hope the reader comes away with information that might one-day help save their lives.

I want to thank Joan Lemley who kept after me to complete this book. You may not be reading this today if it weren't for Joan's help. I enjoyed telling some of the stories of things that happened to me. I still laugh about some of the things that I believe all contributed to my sailing across the ocean and writing this book.

I also want to thank my wife, Judi, who has supported me in all of my endeavors. Without her love and support none of what I have done would have been possible.

*"They are ill discoverers that think
there is no land, when they can see nothing
but sea"*
—*Francis Bacon*

I

Background To Survival

I have told this story hundreds of times. As I tell it to you now, imagine that you, the reader, are in an audience listening to the story unfold as I show slides of my expedition.

I was born in Abilene, Texas, land of oil, cattle, and cotton, but mostly, horizon to horizon, flat, dusty land interspersed with a few low hills. The closest body of water is Fort Phantom Lake, a small, muddy lake ten miles from town, and almost 30 feet deep at the dam, that is, in the rainy season. Thirty feet! To a land-lubber boy, that is, "scary deep!" What mysteries could lurk in those depths, and could a person swim to that deep and live? Such were the thoughts of a kid growing up in West Texas. Though I was never scared of the water, I learned to respect it. When my Dad and I fished on the lake, I was in awe that we could cross such a big body of water in our small, rented fishing boat.

From the first grade until I graduated from McMurry College, I completed all my schooling in Abilene, a true land-locked native son. During the summer months, I worked as a counselor at a YMCA camp. That's where I got my first taste of sailing. Soon, the experience of sailing a 14-foot Sunfish sailboat across Possum Kingdom Lake gave me visions of becoming a world-class sailor. I pictured myself crossing the oceans, visiting exotic foreign ports, winning the America's Cup. I was fascinated by the fact that I could sail for miles and miles for free; no motor, no gas, no noise.

After graduating from college, it was inevitable that I would join the Navy. Along with my interest in sailing, I wanted to become an airline pilot. The world offered unlimited possibilities! The Navy offered me the whole package, sailing around the oceans of the world and flying. They sent me to Aviation Officers Candidate School, (AOCS), in Pensacola, Florida, as a trainee in the Navy's top-rated course in flying. Part of that training included a great course in ocean survival. It was a perfect match for me. Besides being slapped around a little, I actually enjoyed the escape and evasion training the Navy put us through. My interest focused on survival in the wilderness as well as in the ocean. But the ocean interested me far more because it presents such a potentially hostile and challenging environment to us terrestrial beings.

In a particular phase of our ocean survival training, we were dropped off a vessel in Pensacola Bay for a day in the water. When I say, "dropped off," it means literally, "dropped off" into the water from a 20-foot tower built onto the stern of a Navy motor launch. Because we did everything, "the Navy way," we were called to jump off the tower in alphabetical order. Under different circumstances this would have been an advantage for me since my name begins with "S", which would give me plenty of time to study most of the jumpers, and learn from their mistakes as they hit the water. However, on this particular day, the wind chill factor was below freezing. As I stood there waiting my turn, I became extremely cold. My hands got so cold that I could barely feel my fingers. This was going to cause me trouble!

All through Officers Candidate School, and flight training, I became acutely aware of the fact that it wouldn't take much of a slip-up to find myself, or any trainee for that matter, out of the "program." The trigger word was receiving a "down". Two "downs" and you got a "speedy board" which meant you were likely to be removed from the officer and pilot program. Two screw ups and you were out. That put a lot of pressure on each cadet to perform and do everything "by the book".

Because the designated exercise on this training day was

to simulate an actual parachute jump into the sea, harnesses were connected to our parachute straps. In the classroom it was a simple matter to reach up and release the snaps. But here on the cold day of the actual drop, our instructions called for release of the snaps when our feet hit the water. The Navy warned that an early release of the snaps often resulted in crewman injury, the reason being that depth perception is very deceiving over an open body of water. To leave your parachute while still many feet in the air could end in a hard landing on water, and cause severe injury.

My name, "Sigler!" was finally called. By then, I was chilled to the bone as I climbed the tower. The instructor hooked up the parachute straps to my harness as I stood there looking at the froth from the wake of the boat as it sped through the water. Jumping off the boat, and getting pulled through water was supposed to simulate the worst possible conditions, for example, a "downed airman" with an open parachute being dragged across ocean waves in a high wind. My fingers by now were almost frozen; I couldn't feel a thing. Thoughts of "washing out" of flight training right here in survival school ran through my head. Even before it was my turn to jump, I could see that I would have trouble releasing those snaps. Since I'd already lost feeling in my fingers, it could only get worse trying to feel for the snaps while being pulled through the cold water.

When my turn came, there was nothing to do but jump. I hit the water, and it felt surprisingly warm. I remember hearing the sound of the boat's propeller as I sank beneath the surface. Instantly, I was jerked up to the surface, I rolled over on my back as instructed, and tried to release the damn snaps. It was impossible! I couldn't see the snaps while being pulled through the water, and I couldn't feel them with my cold fingers. At that instant I spotted the "safety boat" as it began to move toward me. This could mean in Navy terms that I was "in a world of shit" if the safety diver had to release me. I grabbed the shroud lines, and pulled myself out of the water as far as possible so that I could see when my fingers were on the release snaps. I ran my hand up the lines until I saw my fingers under the snaps. I pushed with all my strength even though I could not feel either the snaps or my fingers. In milliseconds, my last frantic effort paid off. I released both fittings, inflated my life raft, and gave a, "thumbs up" to the safety boat.

We were to spend the remainder of the day in our one-man life rafts. The Navy gave us the normal survival rations, the kind of equipment that would be carried by all naval pilots. Included in the package were, "Charms" candies, a fishing kit, some signal flares, a signal mirror, a knife, some first-aid items, a survival book, a bug net, a whistle, some sunscreen (which promoted rather than protected against sunburn), a compass, a tarp for protection from the elements, a solar still for converting salt water to drinking water, and a survival radio. I looked over these items after crawling into my one-man life raft, and there, in that instant, was created what was to become, for me, a passion for improvement. We floated around Pensacola Bay for a number of hours until a launch came by to pick us up.

There were approximately 70 cadets in my class, large by today's standards. But this was the winter of 1968. Vietnam was heating up, and there was a great demand for pilots.

Because we had all jumped off the speeding boat, we scattered over a wide area of the bay. Surprisingly I warmed up in the raft even though I was soaking wet. I would make note of this. Through with examining the survival equipment, I took out the fishing kit, dropped a line in the water, and set up, "housekeeping." My roommate, Paul Service, (his name in the "S" group next to mine), having jumped just before I, came floating close by. In Navy tradition, all of us had formed a, "betting pool" before our jumps. A prize would be awarded to the person who caught the largest fish. After we were picked up and delivered to dry land, we compared our catches. Imagine everyone's surprise to find that the winning fish was smaller than the bait fish we had purchased.

The life rafts given us for our day in the water were the type carried by the Navy's smaller fighter jet aircraft. They measured a mere five feet by three feet, and there was barely any room to sit. Our knees were close to our chests. Larger Navy and Air Force transport aircraft carry much larger rafts that can hold anywhere from six to twenty people. I was surprised to learn how durable were those little inflatable life rafts, especially if given proper care. During World War II, castaways had managed to stay afloat for months in those small rafts. For this reason, they were to be respected for what they were: inflatables, or merely rubber tubes filled with air.

My first experience with the fragility of those tubes came as we trained on that long day in Pensacola Bay. As I mentioned, my best friend in AOCS, Paul Service, floated by me. He was playing around with the knife from the survival kit. Paul was what we Texans call a, "city slicker," and I could tell he was having a love affair with his knife.

I told Paul, "If he didn't quit fucking around playing with the knife that he would punch a hole in his raft." Well, as fate would have it, Paul dropped the knife. It landed, pointed end down of course, right into the inflation tube. He and his raft began to sink slowly lower and lower into the water. I saved my first life that day. I invited Paul to tie up to my raft for the balance of the day. And I made sure the knife stayed in his sinking raft.

Being a Naval Aviator was one of the biggest kicks I'd had in life. The Madison Avenue promotions for a, "See The World" Navy don't even come close in depicting the real adventure lived by a naval pilot. I flew the A-3 aircraft which was the largest jet operating on a carrier. It was so big that I was able to keep a bicycle in the bomb bay for the times I flew the aircraft to land bases for maintenance or repairs. This is how I met my future wife. On one such trip, I was scheduled to fly from the carrier the USS FDR to Rota, a town on the southern tip of Spain. I was always glad to be catapulted from the ship knowing that I was going to some foreign port for another adventure. When I arrived in Rota, I turned the plane over to the maintenance crew, lowered my bike from the bomb bay and rode off into town. My Spanish had been improving during the two months I'd been in and out of Spain. Nevertheless, when I tried flirting with a Spanish lady now and then, I was still handicapped, to say the least.

On this trip, however, as I was riding back to base after watching fishermen bring in their morning catch I noticed three girls with backpacks sitting on a wall looking at a map. They looked American so I wheeled over to them. I was delighted to find they spoke English. They were Canadian college students on a tour of Europe. One of the girls, Judi, became my wife two years later.

I loved the Navy. Being on a carrier was a great adventure. Once I was almost blown right over the side of the ship as I was crossing the flight deck to get to my airplane. It is hard to describe the noise on the flight deck as 20 or more jet aircraft are all starting, taxiing to the catapults and launching. I was walking across the deck when an A-7 turned to taxi and went to a high power setting blowing me right over. I was sliding across the deck towards the edge grabbing at the tie down loops welded into the flight deck for tying down aircraft. Finally the sailor guiding the A-7 saw what was happening and signaled the A-7 driver to cut power. I stopped just 4 feet from the edge of the flight deck. I got up, manned my aircraft and flew the mission, but I never forgot that lesson.

I still hold the record for the longest non-stop flight for a tactical, carrier-based single piloted aircraft. It was a flight I made from Rota, Spain, to San Francisco in an A-3 when I was in the Naval Reserve. As young naval cadets we were warned that when any sailor began a story with the words, "this is no shit" the story you were about to hear might be suspect of being the whole truth. Well this is no shit. I was in the Naval Reserve and had volunteered to fly an A-3 from Cherry Point Marine Corp Air Station to Rota, Spain acting as emergency tanker and pathfinder for a Marine A-6 Intruder Squadron that was going on to Italy to take part in NATO exercises.

When we got to Rota we were to wait there for 10 days for the A-6's and lead them back across the Atlantic. I liked Rota but I really didn't want to stay there for 10 days. The Marine colonel who was the officer-in-charge of our group and for whom I had worked previously took pity on me, and told me the Marines would pay for 10 hours of flight time on my A-3 if I wanted to fly some. I'm sure he was thinking that I would go out and do field carrier landing practice or something like that remaining in the Rota area. That wasn't my thinking at all. I thanked him, and could hardly contain my excitement. I had a Navy jet in Europe with 10 hours of flight time to use any way I wanted. Because the A-3 crew consisted of a pilot and up to three crewmen, I consulted my crew on this trip which consisted of one enlisted crew chief and an NFO (Naval Flight Officer), Mike Grant, about where they might like to go. The crew chief elected to stay in Rota, and Mike was open to suggestions. I told him I would like to go to Copenhagen in Denmark. Neither of us had ever been there so we got the *Foreign Clearance Guide* out and read about flying to Denmark. Mike was an attorney by profession, and he did not like what he read about flying into Denmark. The guide stated clearly that prior permission was required (PPR) before entering

Denmark airspace, and we had to be on official government business. I didn't have any legal training so those statements didn't bother me nearly as much as they did Mike. I also convinced Mike that I as Pilot-In-Command and Senior Officer was the one responsible and as he was junior to me in rank, I was ordering him to come with me, at least that was my story.

We filed a flight plan to Copenhagen, had the aircraft fueled and took off. Over Germany I got on the radio and called the foreign clearance office located in England. Mike sat in what I am sure was amazement as he listened to what I was telling the clearance office.

A few years prior to this flight I had flown a number of hops out of England to the USS Kennedy a carrier which was on exercises in the North Atlantic. We carried the mail to the ship, picked up the outgoing mail and flew it back to England. On those trips I passed very near the cost of Norway. When operating at sea on carriers, we always tried to have divert bases plotted in case we could not land on the carrier and had to get to the nearest land base. Some of those bases were in Norway.

When we had taken off from Rota I did not know for sure how we would get permission to fly into Denmark, then I remembered my trips carrying mail to the Kennedy. I had my plan, keyed my radio and called, "Clearance, this is Navy 604 Foxtrot calling, over."

"Navy 604 Foxtrot this is military command, over."

"Command this is 604 Foxtrot, we are a Navy A-3 aircraft over Germany on a flight plan to Copenhagen, Denmark and we need a PPR for landing, over."

"Navy 604 Foxtrot understand you are a naval aircraft with a destination of Copenhagen requesting a PPR. What is your ETA Copenhagen, over?"

"Command 604 Foxtrot estimating Copenhagen at 1430 ZULU, over."

"Navy 604 Foxtrot, standby."

Mike and I were excited that all seemed to have gone so smoothly. It looked like we were going to get our clearance, but I was a little scared that the next call might be to deny us clearance, or worst direct us to land and explain what we were up to.

"Navy 604 Foxtrot this is Command, can you tell us the purpose of your flight to Denmark, over?"

It was Showtime! "Command, Navy 604 Foxtrot is a carrier based aircraft inspecting possible emergency carrier "divert" sites in the North Atlantic area and we need to land and check facilities at Copenhagen, over."

"Standby", came the reply.

I began to feel I was getting into a "world of shit" to use a navy expression. Standby, sounded too much like someone was checking out my story. We were screaming over Holland and nearing the Danish boarder at a speed of seven miles a minute when we finally got a call back.

"Navy 604 Foxtrot, Command, over."

"Command, 604 Foxtrot go ahead, over."

"Navy 604 Foxtrot you have been cleared into Danish airspace and your PPR number is Delta 3345, over."

"Roger Command, PPR Delta 3345, Navy 604 Foxtrot, out."

We had done it! We were cleared to Copenhagen.

We landed at the military field and were driven to town by a young Danish Officer who seemed quite amazed that we had come to visit. We had a real tour of Europe. We visited Copenhagen, Amsterdam, and London prior to returning to Rota to lead the A-6's back across the "pond" to Gander, Newfoundland where we were scheduled to land.

On our last night in Rota, Mike and I went downtown to have supper at one of the local pubs. There we ran across the Marine KC130 tanker pilots who would be refueling us the next day as we crossed the Atlantic. As we talked a little shop about the fuel that the A-6's would require, an idea came to me that if I could take all the extra fuel the KC130's might have left over, I could fly non-stop from Rota to San Francisco. I really wanted to get home as it was almost Christmas so not having to stop and overnight in Gander appealed to me. With the help of the Marines and Mike we penned out the flight on bar napkins. Was it even possible?

I told the Marines that if we pulled this off, they would have taken part in the longest flight of a single-piloted carrier based aircraft, a world record. We would all have a place in naval history. I was really trying to sell them on this as I needed their support or my plan would never work. Mike had been busy calculating the flight time it would require to make the flight.

"George, it will take almost 14 hours to make the flight

non-stop counting the speed of the A-6's and the time to slow down to refuel. That will put you at least six hours over the allowable flight time for a single piloted naval aircraft, meaning you will be in violation of navy regs." (regulations)

The tanker pilots didn't mind my being court-martialed and my crew agreed to fly with me because I was senior officer and would take the "hit" for the violation.

Now I loved flying and I didn't want to be driven out of the Navy, but I did want to make the longest flight, a record I knew no one would likely break as it might be a career ending stunt. I weighed the choices. Hell, I was only in the Naval Reserve so worst case scenario would be that I would have to resign my commission and get out of the Navy.

I had been in the Navy long enough to understand the politics of Naval Operations, and I had been reading *Catch 22* during the trip. It occurred to me that if I composed a press release and sent it to all the major news networks that maybe I could just pull this off without ending my career.

I stayed up late composing the release which is printed herein, as it was released to the Navy and the press. The next morning I gave the press release to the Communications Chief in Rota and told him not to put it on the wire until he saw me depart. I figured if the Navy saw the wire before I left they would have to stop me. Once airborne I figured I would "loose" my radios so they couldn't call me back.

The KC130 tankers had taken off early the next morning 4 or 5 hours prior to my departure so as to position themselves on the tanker tracks. Because the KC-130 were turboprops and flew much slower than the jets, they had to leave early to be on station when we caught up with them. We were scheduled to refuel twice over the Atlantic. When we got to Gander, there would be another KC-130 there for emergency purposes in case anyone was running low on fuel.

We "hit" the first tankers, filled our tanks and proceeded on to the next tankers. Everything was going smoothly as we refueled again the second time and proceeded to Gander. Over Gander I had to circle overhead the field until the last A-6 landed, then we took every drop of fuel the Marines had left over. The only hitch on the whole flight was the fact that it was so bumpy over Gander that I almost could not refuel. The "basket" that I had to fly my fuel probe into was moving up and down in a wild 7 to 8 foot motion. The Marine pilot seeing I was having trouble plugging into the basket came on the radio, "604" maybe you would have better luck plugging the basket if we put some hair around it." I appreciated the humor, but I was working my ass off and they were laughing theirs off. Sweat was pouring off me by the time I finally got "plugged" into the tanker. Although I had tanked hundreds of times, day and night, this was a real challenge that I didn't need after having flown for over seven hours.

I had my fuel and the Marines wished me good luck. We flew west over Canada, and arrived at the Naval Air Station after just over 13 hours of flight time. As we landed the control tower advised us not to taxi to our hangar but to the base of the control tower at Base Operations. Taxing in I could see a large crowd gathered in front of Operations and people holding what were obviously TV cameras. Just like *Catch 22* I knew the Navy would either have to court-martial me or make me a hero, so they made me a hero. Although in private I got a chewing out, I had the record, which is remarkable only to the point that anyone would jeopardize their career to get it.

Growing up, I had always thought I wanted to be an airline pilot, but after a few thousand hours of flying in the Navy, I realized that flying a jet from one location to another was really boring to me. While I enjoyed the places a jet could take me, I just didn't get a charge out of simply flying a plane from point A to point B, unlike some other pilots. In order to fly with the airlines, I would have to start as a flight engineer, work up to first officer, then finally, ten years or more later, and if I got lucky, I might make captain. In fact, I have a few ex-navy friends who've been with the airlines for twenty years and who are still not captains. I've told Judi that flying for ten years to get into the command seat of an airliner was like climbing Mount Everest twice. I had already been a designated Pilot-in-Command of a large navy jet aircraft, and I didn't savor spending the next twenty years working my way up to the left seat, the captain's seat, again. After all, I'd already, "been there, done that." Life is too short to do the same thing twice. So I looked to do something different.

After being released from active duty at NAS (Naval Air Station) Alameda after my tour in Vietnam, I began to think about another career. My home base had been NAS Alameda, California, on San Francisco Bay, so I decided to stay around there, and I married Judi Lightfoot the Canadian jewel I had met in Spain on my first tour of duty. We couldn't afford a home so I purchased a houseboat, and we lived in Alameda at Barnhill's Marina across the estuary from Jack London Square which was in Oakland.

Still intrigued with water, sailing, and boats, I decided to try and get a job in the marine business. I joined a Naval Reserve A-3 Squadron at NAS Alameda in order to put bread on the table while I searched for a chance to change my career from aviation to boating. But try as I might, there was not a decent position in the marine field to be had. Or any position, for that matter. The bare fact was converse: that even though I had a career in the Navy, I knew nothing about the marine business.

Providentially, I came across a book that changed my life. It was, *Survive the Savage Sea*, by Dougal Robertson. Robertson was an experienced sailor from Britain, who, with his family and a friend, was sailing his yacht around the world. While sailing in the Pacific Ocean near the Galapagos Islands, their boat was violently struck by a whale. Robertson realized, when he saw the ocean gushing into his yacht that she was going to sink very quickly. He had made sparse preparation for ocean survival even though his experience at sea was considerable. His life raft was an old leaking mess. His survival kit was not well thought out, and the location of the life-saving equipment made it difficult to off-load from boat to life raft.

Robertson's yacht sank very quickly. Within a few minutes she was gone. After drifting for a few days, and hoping for rescue, Robertson finally realized that the only way they were going to survive would be to rig a sail on their dinghy, and attempt to sail east to the coast of South America. They sailed thirty-seven days before they were seen and rescued by a ship. Robertson had been ill-equipped for survival, but he made up for his lack of preparation by developing a plan of action, i.e., setting sail for land.

After reading his book, I realized that I knew more about ocean survival than Robertson did. I became convinced that I could develop a survival kit that would save lives. With this thought, I became really excited about going into business for myself. I would make survival kits that would save lives. It never occurred to me that there was a very limited market for

survival kits as there were few people actually sailing and flying small aircraft and boats across the ocean. I just knew I
could produce a product that would save lives.

Immersing myself in reading accounts of disasters at sea,
I read thousands of stories about castaways. I borrowed information from Captain Bligh since he had one of the greatest
stories ever written about saving himself and his men.
Important, life-saving lore in Bligh's story concerns the knowledge of temperature differences and evaporation. Bligh and
his men were caught in a cold, driving rain while sailing their
small life boat across the South Pacific. His men became cold-
soaked. Bligh ordered his men to soak their clothing in salt
water which would make them warmer. First, the sea water
was warmer than the rain water there in the tropics of the
South Pacific, and secondly, Bligh knew that sea water evapo-
rated less quickly than fresh rain water. The law of physics
applies to the rate of evaporation. A slower rate of evaporation
lessens the air-conditioning, or cooling effect, of evaporative
cooling. Today, we know this to be an important point in the
prevention of hypothermia.

I borrowed further from Thor Heyerdahl's book, *Kon
Tiki*, an account of his crossing the Pacific Ocean in a raft built
from trees. Heyerdahl was not on a survival expedition, but
had set out to prove that the South Pacific Islanders may have
come from South America. I made note that on occasion,
Heyerdahl and his men often poured a little sea water into
their drinking water when they were thirsty. He and his men
realized that the feeling of thirst is not always quenched by
drinking purified water absent of minerals. Adding a little sea
water, with its minerals, to pure or distilled water relieved
their thirst. Simply put, sea water with its high mineral content mixed with fresh water was more thirst-quenching than
pure, distilled water.

Overall, I read more than three-thousand accounts of
castaways. Some can only be described as tragic, while others
were truly heroic. The tragedy is that these were the accounts
of the survivors. The many more who didn't make it to safety
would never tell their stories. For every person who survived
a disaster at sea, there were ten times that many who didn't
live to tell their stories.

I spent hundreds of hours in the Oakland library doing
survival research. In fact, my survival kit would be developed

as a result of research in this very library. I kept notes of what survivors had to say about their experiences. If a particular remedy or action helped a person to survive, or they mentioned a need for some item that was lacking, I made a note of it. Especially intriguing was an account of items packaged into survival kits that would have actually hastened death rather than prolonged life!

It was shocking to read about what I considered basic survival knowledge, but knowledge that was apparently unknown to the castaways who wrote their stories. After reading these thousands of accounts, I gleaned the foundation for what I knew would be the, "world's best ocean survival kit." All my research was written on hundreds of 3 X 5 index cards which, when compiled, would lead me to a most needed, and well thought-out survival kit.

Before launching into my story of sailing a rubber, inflatable boat from San Francisco to Hawaii, to prove my survival kit, it is necessary here to describe my methodology for assembling the survival gear, and the rationale behind what came to be known as the, "Sig II Survival Kit."

The major reason for my finally writing this book is the fact that the information is still as relevant today as it was twenty years ago or a thousand years ago. The physiology of the human body has changed very little over the span of thousands of years. Also, I have recently read other books written by castaways who would have profited from the knowledge I gained from my research.

For my research into survival at sea, one book in particular stands alone, and besides, makes very enjoyable reading. It is Doctor Alain Bombard's, *Le Hertique*. Dr. Bombard was a French physician who did a great deal of study in human survival. In fact, he went so far as to proclaim that a castaway could literally live off the ocean. The doctor went to great lengths to prove his theories eventually by floating a rubber inflatable boat from Europe to the Caribbean Islands. He ate fish, collected plankton, etc., for food. When there was little rain, he used a fruit squeezer to squeeze fluid out of fish flesh. Dr. Bombard also supplemented his drinking water by drinking sea water. His ideas were radical, so consequently never were accepted for what they were. His detractors diluted the original reasons for his experiments. He had seen many castaways who had died for what seemed to be no apparent physical reason.

Bombard had been involved in ocean rescue operations during World War II where there were many survivors, but many who died for what seemed to him no apparent reason. Those who died did not seem to have any debilitating physical problems that would explain their deaths. He concluded that many people died in ocean disasters because they gave up the will to live. He theorized that the reality of being alone in the ocean with little chance of rescue was an overpowering mental obstacle with which they could not deal. He believed that many castaways, knowing they could not drink sea water, and left with little or no food available, simply gave up the will to survive. I came to appreciate that desperate feeling many years later when I ditched an aircraft I was flying to Australia 600 miles south of Hawaii.

While in the Navy Reserves, a pilot friend of mine had asked me if I would be interested in flying a Cessna single engine aircraft from Oakland to Sydney, Australia. I was surprised to learn that there were pilots out there that flew these small aircraft across the ocean on a routine basis. It sounded exciting, so I took him up on the offer since the pay wasn't bad, and I needed the extra money. I became what is known as a "ferry pilot". I ferried small aircraft all over the world. Flights across the ocean in single engine piston driven aircraft certainly have built-in risk. I lost a few friends to that kind of work, but there was a certain amount of adventure that drew me to it. The flights themselves were long monotonous journeys, but landing on, and seeing all the little islands of the South Pacific was more than worth it.

In order for the small aircraft to make it on the long over water flights they are equipped with fuel tanks that are installed inside the cabin where the seats have been removed. A typical flight in a small Cessna might take between 13 to 18 hours from San Francisco to Hawaii compared to a 5-hour flight in an airliner. But ferry pilots make these flights on a daily basis. If the reader happens to be reading this book flying across the Atlantic or Pacific, there is surely a ferry pilot flying just a few thousand feet above the ocean going 140 MPH, slowly making his or her way across the same route hoping their one engine keeps running.

Ironically, the one time I had to ditch an airplane into the ocean I was flying a Cessna 310 which has two engines. I was hired by a young Australian doctor, Miles Connell, who owned the plane to fly it from Oakland to Hay, Australia. He asked me if he might fly back with me. I was a little surprised because of the risk involved, but he was young and said he needed some adventure in his life. Seems that Hay was a small town in the "outback" and he wanted this plane so he could fly to Sydney to party and meet some women. I agreed that he could come along since it was his airplane. But I told him that flying a small aircraft across the ocean was fraught with some degree of risk.

I shared with Miles a story of my flying a Cessna 210 single engine airplane to Australia a few months before. I was scheduled to pick up the 210 in Oakland and fly it to Darwin, Australia. I planned the flight from Oakland to Hawaii, then west to Majuro in the Marshall Islands. From there I would fly to Guadacanal in the Solomon Islands, across the Coral Sea to Cairns, and then on to Darwin.

The Cessna was equipped with the nicest electronics I had ever seen in a small aircraft, and it had a great auto pilot which would relieve me of having to hand fly the plane the entire trip. The pre flight planning went smoothly but I made note of the fact that there was forecast to be 40 knots of wind on the ocean surface for the first few hundred miles of the trip, and there would be isolated thunderstorms along the route of flight. The wind would only be a concern if I ditched the plane, and I had a storm scope that could guide me around thunderstorms. I figured that the flight should take about 14 hours, but I had fuel enough to fly almost 20 hours.

Early the next morning I fueled the plane and taxied out for take off. The flight went smoothly until I had just passed the "point of no return", that point at which I could only make it to Hawaii instead of turning around and flying back to California. I was just about half way between Hawaii and California or just over a thousand miles from either place; right in the middle of the Pacific.

I began to smell smoke. Something was burning! Fire in an aircraft is a situation that no pilot wants to confront. It smelled like electrical wire burning so I turned off all the unnecessary electrical equipment. The trick is to isolate the system that has shorted and then leave it off or pull the circuit breaker to that system. I slowly began to turn on the necessary equipment one at a time, waiting a few minutes to see if any circuit breakers popped or if I smelled the fire again. Finally I had everything back on and smelled no fire. I couldn't see the ampere meter because the fuel tank next to me covered the instrument panel on the right side of the aircraft.

I was uncomfortable at best, because I knew I had smelled smoke but now everything seemed fine. What the hell had burned? About 30 minutes later I made a position report, but I noticed that the transmissions sounded somewhat fuzzy. I then noticed that my digital VHF radio displays were blank. My clock which took very little power had stopped working. I was loosing all electrical power!

I was not too worried about navigating with no instruments, but I realized that I would be flying at night and would have no lights other than my flashlight. I tried to call and report the fact that I was loosing my radios and proceeding on to Hawaii, but I could no longer transmit. I was now forced to hand fly the plane as the autopilot was electrically driven and had failed.

In theory, the fuel in the ferry tanks which were inside the cockpit with me were suppose to transfer via ram air pressure through the electrical fuel pump to the engine. I was flying at 6000 feet still evaluating my options and course of action when the engine just quit. No warning at all, it just stopped. I put the plane in a slight dive to maintain airspeed, and switched the fuel from the ferry tanks to the main tanks located in the wings of the airplane, which are above the cockpit on the 210 and above the engine. The engine started again as gravity pulled the fuel to the engine. The problem was I did not have enough fuel in the wing tanks to make it to Hawaii.

I stabilized the plane and switched back to the ferry tanks. Again the engine quit. I quickly switched back to wing fuel, and the engine started again. I was in a real dilemma, the engine would not run with the ferry fuel selected, and I couldn't make it to Hawaii without the ferry fuel. I climbed back to 6000 feet and thought that perhaps if I pulled the power back a little and slowed down that the corresponding demand for less fuel by the engine would make it possible for the ferry tanks to keep it running. Again the engine quit. I was quickly running out of ideas. I couldn't make a MAYDAY call because I had no radios. I couldn't make it to Hawaii on the wing fuel alone. All I could do was continue toward Hawaii.

I had to figure out a way to get the ferry fuel to the

engine; find a way to force the fuel out of the tanks. I needed some way to pressurize the fuel tanks. I had tools with me that I always carried on a ferry flight to make minor repairs. I had my life raft which I kept handy in case of emergencies. It dawned on me that the raft had a hand pump in it that I might somehow use to plumb pressure into the ferry tanks forcing the fuel to the engine.

I pulled the life raft out and found the hand pump. I also had the two things in my tool bag that will repair almost any airplane, bailing wire and duct tape. Now came the tricky part. I had to get out of my seat and turn around backwards to get to the fuel cap on the back ferry tank. The trick was to fly the plane while turned backwards. I unscrewed the fuel cap from the ferry tank and wrapped duct tape around the hose from the hand pump until it was as large as the opening to the fuel tank. I forced the hose into the tank cap as hard as I could so that no air would escape. I then sat back in my seat and started pumping with my right hand while flying the plane with my left.

I switched the fuel from the wing tanks to the ferry tanks, all the while pumping. The engine kept running! I was still flying at reduced power so I let well enough alone. It would take me longer to get to Hawaii that way, but it least now I had a chance to get there. I did not want to ditch as the wind was blowing so hard on the ocean, that the ocean surface looked white.

Now, however, I had another couple of problems. If I stopped pumping for more than 10 to 15 seconds the engine quite again. I still had at least 8 hours and probably more to fly at the reduced airspeed. I couldn't continue to fly, pump, and navigate so I had to switch to wing fuel occasionally in order to have one hand free to plot my position and determine a course of action. I was flying using the wet compass which was OK but not nearly as accurate as the gyro compass which was inoperative. I knew that the Big Island of Hawaii was closer than Oahu, so I plotted a new course to the Big Island. I was now strictly using DR (Dead Reckoning) for navigation. I had to guess my ground speed and fly time and distance. I had a wrist watch and a wet compass so I could navigate. I just hoped the wind forecast I received on pre flight was accurate. At my new, slower speed it was going to take another 9 hours to get to Hawaii.

I sat up a routine of pumping for about 30 minutes until my arm became numb then switched to the wing fuel so I could rest. I was working so hard that I soon drank all the water and soda I had brought along. My mouth became dry and sweat poured off me. Hour after hour dragged by. "How could it get any worse?" I asked myself. I shouldn't have asked.

Up ahead I could see the thunderstorms that had been predicted. I could see heavy rain under the clouds that were towering above me. I didn't want to fly through any thunderstorms or clouds for two reasons: First it is never a good idea to fly through a thunderstorm because the air currents can cause sever damage to an aircraft and loss of control; secondly, I had no attitude gyro to help me keep the wings level.

I had to note how long and how many degrees I deviated from my course in order to fly around a storm and then make the correction back to my original course. I climbed over some clouds and flew under others. Sometimes I could just not avoid flying through the clouds. At first flying through the clouds with few instruments was a challenge, but then I began to get use to it. By flying through the clouds I could stay on my course making my trip that much shorter.

After a few hours the pumping was wearing me out. I was becoming really mad at the airplane. All that nice equipment and nothing worked. The sun worked its way west and I was following it, but I was moving at 120 knots and it was traveling away from me at 420 knots, and soon it began to set.

Dark was not good. I now had to fly with my flash light either taped to my head or in my teeth. As it got dark, I could not tell whether or not I was flying into clouds. Now I was pumping, navigating, holding a flashlight, and flying the plane on partial panel. Because my wing fuel gauges did not work, I had to keep track of how long I had burned fuel out of each tank, as I didn't want my engine to quit at night.

At about 9 o'clock that night I saw a light on the water. I was totally worn out, physically and mentally. I descended down to 500 feet and flew over the light. It was a sailboat heading east. I considered ditching the plane next to the yacht, as I didn't know how much further Hawaii was. After navigating for hours using DR, I wasn't positive of my position and I wasn't sure of how much fuel I had left.

I was brought back to reality when the engine quit almost

right over the yacht. I had stopped pumping, becoming fixated on the yacht. I switched to the wing tanks and the engine came back to life. I started a climb and decided to continue on west. I wondered to myself what the people in the yacht must have thought about a plane flying over them at night with the engine quitting.

I climbed back up to 6000 feet and again was in and out of clouds. The moon was out, however, and it gave me a relatively steady fix to fly by. It was almost impossible to follow the wet compass at night as I had to shine the light on it time and again. With the moon, I could check my compass heading and then keep the moon in the same relative position and maintain heading that way which was a big improvement.

I had flown for almost sixteen and a half hours. I was beginning to think I may have missed Hawaii. I strained to see any lights ahead or to the side. I checked and rechecked my DR. I just could not believe that I could have flown over Hawaii and not seen it, but if my forecast winds were not accurate and I was being pushed north or south, I could be way off course.

I continued west. Lights! I could see lights. Not more than 60 miles away directly ahead. I had switched to the wing tanks after my incident with the sailboat because I figured if I was anywhere close to accurate I had enough fuel left in the wing tanks to get me to Hawaii. I focused on the lights. I could see more lights. I was still in and out of the clouds but I was flying directly toward the lights.

As I neared the lights, I thought I might have to land on a road as I had no idea which island I was over. I looked down between the clouds and saw the bright lights of a runway. By dumb luck I was directly above an airport. I began a descending turn through the clouds keeping my eye on the runway. I still had to be careful. I was talking to no one, had no exterior lights, and here I was getting ready to land at what was obviously a substantial airport. There could be airliners and other small aircraft in the air.

I set up for landing. I had the field made, but the airplane had one more surprise for me. The engine quit. I switched tanks but noting happened. I didn't have time to do anything but concentrate on the landing. "What else could happen?" I thought. I didn't have to wait long for the answer. I reached over and put the landing gear handle down. Nothing happened! "Shit", I though to myself, I had no electrical power to drive the hydraulic pump. I had to pump the gear down with the emergency gear handle. I did some inspired pumping, and the gear came down as I rolled out for final approach. I touched down and rolled off the runway on to the grassy infield. I was still concerned that no one knew I was there, and that an airliner might land on top of me. I slumped in the seat. I was beat. My right arm was hurting so badly that I could barely move it.

A truck with the airport manager came out, and he said that they had been watching me on radar as I neared Hawaii and had cleared the air space so that I could land. He informed me I was on Maui. He asked if I needed anything. "Water and aspirin," I replied.

I thought Miles would run the other way when he heard that story, but I think it had the opposite effect, and he saw this as even more of an adventure. The Cessna 310 Miles had purchased was a fine looking aircraft. I actually looked forward to flying this plane to Australia. Besides that, Miles was a pilot and could help me with the flying.

We flew from Oakland to Kona, Hawaii on the Big Island in just under 12 hours. The flight was uneventful, and the airplane was fast compared to the small single engine ones I had been flying. We stayed the night in Kona and planned to fly down to Pago Pago in Somoa the next day. Because of the long legs of each flight, the plane had lots of fuel on board which made it much heavier than normal. The 310 is designed to carry six passengers, but the fuel weight was the equivalent of having 14 passengers.

We departed Kona early in the morning and had flown about three and a half hours when I felt a jolt from the plane. I thought that we might have hit a bird, but when I looked out the right window I got the shock of my life. I could see oil and engine parts coming out of the cowling. I turned back north towards Hawaii and declared an emergency on the high frequency radio. In an airliner, if you loose an engine and have to get down to landing weight, the pilot can dump fuel to lighten the load. But I could not dump any of the fuel, and the plane was too heavy to maintain flight. I slowly began a descent towards what was a rather disturbed sea. I felt sorry for Miles, but all I could do was remain calm and fly the plane. The engine had failed at 8,000 feet, and I had hoped while descending, at least until I got to a 1000 feet above the ocean, that the plane would sustain altitude. After we passed 1000 feet I knew we were going to end up in the ocean, and I began to slow the plane to determine how slowly I could fly while still maintaining control.

I had been able to confirm our position to the Coast Guard, but I realized that it was a big ocean and finding us, even if we survived the ditching unhurt, would be no small task. I gave my last radio call at 150 feet above the ocean as I now needed to give all my attention to ditching the airplane. Believe it or not, I did not give up totally on the plane continuing to fly until we actually hit the water. The wind on the ocean surface of 40 knots had blown the sea state to 20-foot swells and breaking waves. The "textbook" recommended procedure for ditching was to land the plane parallel to the waves. However, as I looked at the sea conditions I became very concerned that a wing tip could catch on a wave and spin us just prior to impact. I didn't like the idea of spinning into the ocean totally out of control. I could maintain control of the aircraft flying as slow as 60 knots. I could remember falling on water skis going at least 30 knots when I was a kid, so I decided that if I few directly into the waves and wind that my relative speed at impact would be less than 20 knots. I didn't bother calculating the wave speed as it was a non-factor in that I knew the plane would likely bounce off the water and be slowed by impact before we might run directly into the side of a wave. I just had to try and keep the nose as high as possible so we did bounce instead of plow right into a wave.

Right up until the time we hit the water I couldn't believe this was happening to me. But reality set in quickly. We hit the first wave with a bang and bounced to the next wave. I remember seeing the prop from the good engine break off and go skipping off across the top of the water in front of us. Water then covered the windscreen as we drove through the next wave. I was hoping that the plane would not nose under a wave and start sinking quickly. So much water came over the plane that I thought for a moment that we had plowed into a wave and were being driven under water. But the forward motion stopped quickly, and we were floating nicely on top of the water.

I was half scared to move for fear that I would discover than I was injured. I looked at the doctor and asked if he were ok. He said he thought so, and I was amazed to find that neither of us had even a scratch. We exited the plane, and I inflated the small life raft. This raft was round in shape, and I knew it could not be sailed so saving ourselves was out of the question. I had, however, packed an extra emergency locator beacon that I had purchased just prior to leaving Oakland. The plane, which floated for 45 minutes, also had an emergency beacon installed that was designed to activate automatically upon impact.

It is hard to describe the feeling I had sitting in that life raft. One goes from the warm safety of the aircraft with a mind set that you will be having a nice hot dinner on a tropical island, to a cold hostile environment with huge waves crashing down and nothing but water for hundreds of miles. To top off my discouragement, the light on the emergency locator beacon was not working which meant that the beacon might not be putting out a signal. I knew that it would be almost impossible for anyone to find us if the beacon were not working. It would be hard to see us in these sea conditions, and there was a low overcast above us. I was more concerned of dying in that small life raft after two hours than I ever was in the 56 days it took me to cross the Pacific 13 years before. I can tell you that the thought of death is very real. I pictured myself floating in this stupid round raft until I died. Miles was very discouraged and became sea sick which made it even worse for him. And to add to Miles' mental condition was the fact that he had never had much occasion to be near a large body of water, and now he was in the largest body of water in the world. In that situation, it was easy for me to see why some people would give up the will to live. It is extremely discouraging in that there is almost nothing one can do to help one's self. You can't just get out and walk to safety. You can't get warm. You can't avoid the force of the breaking waves. You are stuck in miles of water you can't drink.

I was, however, thankful for one thing. We had plenty of drinking water. It rained so hard that we had to bail water out of the raft. I knew from experience that water was the most critical need we would have for survival, but I had to balance how much water we could sit in, against how cold we might become sitting in the water. I saved as much water as possible, and told the doctor to drink as much as possible. I could not believe that I had once crossed this same ocean for 56 days without receiving one drop of rain, and here I was bailing water out of this life raft.

Dying in a life raft can be a very slow death. You feel totally alone, even though other people may be sharing the same raft with you. I did not think it necessary to tell Miles that the emergency beacon might not be working. It was about 10 AM when we ditched. About 3 o'clock in the afternoon I heard what I knew was a turboprop aircraft high above us. Due to the low overcast I could not see the plane, but I was sure it was a Coast Guard C-130. I traced the sound from north to south until I could no longer hear it. The plane had flown over us, but had continued south. This was not good. I felt that if our beacon had been working he would have turned around as soon as he realized he had over-flown us. About 20 minutes later I again heard the sound of a turbo prop, but now it was louder and much closer. I knew we were a small target on a big ocean. I had flares, but they were useless unless the plane could see the surface. I spread sea dye around us to color the blue water with a dark yellow stain that gave a larger target area. The noise was coming closer, and it was circling above the clouds. I followed the sound with my eyes. The pilot was going to have to descend into and below the low overcast in order to see us. This can be uncomfortable far out to sea, as there was no way for the pilot to know how low the cloud layer was above the ocean surface, and a descent into the ocean was a real possibility if one were not careful.

I had a flare in hand just in case the aircraft was sighted. There it was! The plane was descending out of the clouds not more than one half mile away. It was beautiful! I lit the flare. Someone on the plane must have seen it, as the plane turned right toward us. It flew over us banking its wings back and forth. We were waving like crazy.

As the plane flew over I could see that the back ramp was open, and I could see people standing there. I realized that they were preparing to drop us some equipment and probably a larger life raft. The plane descended even more as it made a wide turn and then came toward us just downwind of our position. Just before it got to us, I saw the equipment come tumbling out. It was tied together with a long rope and hit the water with a zing.

We quickly drifted over the floating rope and gathered in the equipment. I inflated the raft they had dropped which was big enough for 30 people. We climbed into the raft, and I located an emergency radio in a bag and called the C-130 to let them know we were doing fine. I didn't know how we might be rescued, but at least they knew where we were, and we now had lots of food, water, and clothing. I knew Miles felt a lot better now so I tried a little humor.

"Doc, is this enough excitement for you? We lost an engine, ditched the plane, your plane sank, and here we are in the middle of the ocean in a life raft. Is that enough excitement for you so far?" I asked trying to keep a straight face. He could only muster a smile, as he was still very sea sick.

The Coast Guard told me that there was a German freighter about 400 miles south of us heading to Australia that could pick us up in a few days. I responded, "that sounded fine as we didn't have any other travel plans." However, when it got dark the Coast Guard aircraft spotted lights on the water much closer to us. They found a Japanese fishing boat about 40 miles south of our position. That boat was directed to us and picked us up early the next morning. As luck would have it, the boat was going back to Hawaii, and we would be there in three days. The point of telling this story is to emphasis what Dr. Bombard believed, that the will to live can suffer greatly at sea in a life raft.

Dr. Bombard proposed to prove to people that they could live almost indefinitely on what was in the ocean; that a castaway could gain confidence, be resourceful, and stay alive until help comes. He wanted to prove that one could live off the ocean. He did that, but he also had the help of a swim mask, fins, spear, and his fruit squeezer. The fins were for swimming around his raft, in order to spear fish, and the squeezer was used to force water from the flesh.

In most tropical areas of the world, typical of locations where a recreational sailor might find himself, I would say that life could be maintained from 8 to 12 days without water, and from 40 to 60 days without food. There are so many variables involved, one of them is having the education to do everything right in order to live the longest time possible. That education is what this book is about.

"What shall we tell you?
Tales, marvelous tales
Of ships and stars and isles
Where good men rest.
—James E. Flecker

II

Planning The Survival Kit

People who know me, know that I love to eat. In fact, when I'm kidded about being overweight, I tell people that I'm bulking up for an emergency. Because of my love for food, I will describe first what a person might consider when faced with a survival situation, or when packing or buying a survival kit. However, in most ocean survival situations, the lack of drinking water is going to be the most important factor in whether people live or die.

Previously, I mentioned Dr. Bombard and his survival theories because, when I researched the data, I had to know how long a person could live with little or no food, and what kinds of food a castaway would need. My entire philosophy about ocean survival revolved around the castaway saving himself, totally independent of outside help. This meant that a sailor or aviator would have to have a life raft that could be rigged with some sort of sail. For the sailor, a dinghy equipped with a sail would suffice. For the aviator, the weight problem makes it almost impossible to carry a raft with sailing capability. An aviator, however, is usually in radio contact, or is required to be in radio contact if he is over water and beyond a specified distance from land. If he goes down, he can transmit a position, declare, "MAYDAY", or key his microphone with an, "SOS", in code, or activate his ELT (Electronic Locator Transmitter) on the way down. The boater's situation is much different than the pilot's. The boater is probably not on a, "float plan," nor does he have his radio on all the time. Should disaster strike, the boater might find his radio useless, which has happened many times.

I was positive that I could not make a survival kit small enough to keep a person alive indefinitely, so I had to establish some operating parameters. First of all I wanted to make the survival kit small enough so that it could be packed with a life raft in the life raft container. The ideal place for the survival kit was for it to be packed with the life raft.

Next, I had to establish some sort of time marker that was based on how long I needed to keep a person alive. I had to solve a time/distance problem. From research, I learned the approximate speed a person could average sailing a life raft. That speed was about 2 miles an hour. Taking the worst case scenario, I plotted the absolutely furthest point from land in every ocean that a person might find themselves, and found that no point in any ocean was over 2000 miles from some point of land. So if a person sank in that worst case, and using my 2 MPH speed, it would take just over 41 days to make landfall. But alas, a life raft with no keel could not sail a direct route. The castaway might have to sail further than 2000 miles. I came to discover that a castaway confined to a life raft and remaining relatively inactive could expect to live from 40 to 60 days with no food. So using simple math, if a person could sail 48 miles a day, in 40 to 60 days that person could sail between 1900 and 2880 miles. I settled on making a kit that would keep a person alive for at least 60 days.

The extra mileage would help cover the distance that might be necessary in some circumstances. It is possible that a boat might sink 50 miles off a coast with the prevailing winds blowing offshore and make it impossible for the castaway to sail toward that coast. This has happened more than once.

The next problem with which to deal was the determination of the length of time a person could expect to live with no food or water or what I call the zero point. This part of my research was an area about which there was not a lot of information. But, having been a navy pilot, and having remained in the Naval Reserve in order to maintain a living, it dawned on me that I might have a reliable source of information right at my finger tips, the Oakland Naval Hospital! I called the hospital and talked with a doctor in the Clinical Investigation Unit. I asked, "How long could a person expect to live without food?" The doctor was fascinated with my question, but didn't have viable answers. I would have to do more research, and find the answers myself, but my contact with the doctors at the Naval Hospital would prove helpful later.

There was literature on prisoners who had gone on hunger strikes for periods of up to 40 days, but not much medical information accompanied these cases, and left unanswered whether or not the strikers had survived on just water, or had they been supplied with vitamins or some other kinds of nourishment. There were prisoners of war who were confined for long periods with little food or water, but again I could not document what or how much they had to eat. There were some experiments conducted in Germany during the wars that document some rather cruel studies involving starvation, which I used to some extent, but those circumstances involved other hardships that a castaway would not be faced with.

Finally, extrapolating from the best information available and reading more books on nutrition, I determined that most people could expect to live from 40 to 60 days with no food, if they remained in a basal, or resting state. Bear in mind that I was considering castaways in a life raft, not someone in a desert or mountain survival situation who might require energy i.e. food stuff to walk. Therefore, since I had set my target goal for keeping a person alive for 60 days, I calculated that a survival kit would really require little or no food. However, there was the very real psychological factor that doctor Bombard had eluded to that might affect the castaways mental well being if they discovered that their survival kit had no food or rations. Therefore, for more psychological reasons rather than physiological reasons did I pack any food into the survival kit.

What to pack became the next hurdle. There are three basic food groups from which to choose: carbohydrates, fats/oils, and proteins. I quickly eliminated proteins when I found that protein foods such as meats, or jerky, take more water to digest and eliminate than any other food group. A startling fact in my research was that many ocean survival packs, even those for commercial vessels, had dried meats and other protein rich foods packed as their rations. Of course, if a life boat had to be rowed to landfall, those persons rowing would need protein and other energy foods. But then again they would need more water in order for the body to process the protein. In most ocean survival situations, protein type foods would hasten death rather than prolong life. And in consideration of the lack of water for digestion of such protein, the problem becomes even more complicated.

Of course, if I were packing a survival kit for a mountain trip or desert expedition, I might pack some protein. Hiking out of a survival situation, the protein could be a welcome addition to a diet. I decided that an ocean survival pack did not require protein. In addition, almost all sea creatures are good sources of protein, and I intended to pack in the survival kit means of getting fish and other sea animals. And the body could draw upon its own protein in consuming itself.

Next, I considered fats and oil. I liked the idea of carrying fats/oil because per weight they have twice the calories of carbohydrates, and the more calories, the better for the castaway. A pound of hard candy might have 1700 calories, whereas a pound of oil might have over 4000 calories. There was, however, a major drawback to fats/oils; they tend to become rancid. Bacteria infiltrate fats/oils, thus making them a potential danger in eating. I also had to assume that anything packed in a survival kit might be stored for years. I couldn't take the chance with fats and oils. And like protein, sea animals could provide fats, and the body could burn its own fats in a survival situation.

However, in planning a survival kit for myself, and assuming my departure date was near, I would visit my local drug store to buy some wheat germ oil for survival rations. Vitamin E in wheat germ retards bacteria activity thereby creating a relatively long shelf life, at least for an oil. Mountain climbers who want a lot of energy, and little additional pack weight, often pack oils because of their high calories and compact packaging. However, climbers report that when oils get cold, for instance, above 14,000 feet, they are not so easily digested.

Carbohydrates would then remain as the survival food of choice. As mentioned previously, oils generally have twice the amount of calories per weight as do carbohydrates, but the calories in carbohydrates are stable, i.e., they can be stored for long periods of time. Carbohydrates are also an excellent choice for a number of other reasons. There is difficulty in obtaining carbohydrates from the open ocean, although Dr. Bombard was able to collect phyto-plankton which, as a plant, provided him with some carbohydrate manufactured right in the ocean. A net could be packed in a survival kit, but few castaways mentioned that plankton was encountered often enough to be a significant food source. Again, conservation of energy is a must in an ocean survival situation. In my opinion, the energy expended in the collection of plankton would have to be balanced against its value as nourishment.

Carbohydrates have another unique property that appealed to me. They require very little water for digestion, and can be metabolized by the body very easily. In fact, some carbohydrates such as glucose, can be used by the body cells directly. Unfortunately, I managed to escape from high school and college with having taken only two chemistry courses, so my explanations may offend some chemists or biologists, but it was a chemist who explained the following to me, so read on.

Carbohydrates are made up of long chains of carbon molecules with hydrogen atoms and carbon atoms making up the specific type of carbohydrate. When metabolized by the body, the carbon atoms are used as fuel, and the hydrogen atoms are free to join free oxygen atoms in the blood stream to form H_2O, water! Hallelujah! A food that forms molecules of water! This sounded great! My first question was, "If I pack enough candy, would I even need water?" That, however, is not the case. Candy will indeed break down and form water molecules, but not enough to displace the metabolic process itself. Still, the candy would not take as much water to digest as would other food groups.

Fats and proteins can be obtained from birds, fish, turtles, and other organisms in the ocean, but carbohydrates are not to be found in this group. If I elected to pack carbohydrates, it could mean that any castaway with a little fishing luck might secure a rounded diet of carbohydrate, fat, and protein. This was great news to me. All I had to do now was find the right carbohydrate.

For years the Navy has packed hard, sucrose candy as a survival ration in their life rafts. In fact, I've had candy out of a 30-year old survival kit, and it still tasted fine. Carbohydrates come in many different forms: breads, fruits, cakes, candy, syrup, liquids, etc. They also come in a variety of chemical make-ups. Many people have asked me why I didn't pack glucose as a survival ration since it can be absorbed directly by body cells. The actual reason is economy. It was less expensive to pack a sucrose candy than pure glucose. Furthermore, I wasn't ready to explore the reasons why someone might need a direct glucose fix.

Early into my research, I decided that the main point of my project was to make a survival kit that would sustain a person's life for 60 days. I didn't care so much that a castaway might be uncomfortable, or suffer with some minor after-effect, I simply wanted to keep that person alive for 60 days.

My premise that a castaway would most likely be able to supplement his diet with fish, turtle, or birds was borne out in most of the literature written by, and of, castaways. Castaways in almost all of the cases I read about had some luck in that area. However, I did not wish to be absolute in surmising that all castaways would have the capability to supplement their diets with creatures from the ocean. I would consider myself negligently optimistic to assume that every castaway would have the opportunity to find those ocean foods, so I decided merely to pack candy into the survival kit. As the reader will see later, I was right in not counting on food obtained from the ocean.

Most adult males require from 1800 to 2200 calories a day in order to maintain body weight. Females require from 1500 to 1800 calories. That's a hell of a lot of candy to pack! It was a "given" that the castaway was going to lose weight on my diet. In fact, I found through research and my own experience, that after 30 days without food, a castaway's weight loss will average a pound a day, or 30 pounds. These are not rock-hard numbers because few castaways are weighed when they are picked up or knew their exact weight when they fell into a survival situation. The number of pounds lost is determined from my own experience, and those documented cases of persons on hunger strikes.

Using the number of a "pound a day after 30 days", I theorized that I would weigh about 125 pounds if I were adrift for

60 days. I weighed 185 pounds; minus the loss of one pound a day, I would weigh 125 pounds after 60 days. This figure is calculated for men. Women may not drop so fast because their metabolism is slower. Children will drop faster than either men or women because their metabolism is faster. Older people's weight will drop less quickly than younger people because the body's metabolism slows with age. So a woman of 120 pounds would not necessarily lose 60 pounds in 60 days. There is not much documentation to support my mathematics here, but a woman might lose closer to three-quarters of a pound a day, so a woman of 120 pounds could lose 45 pounds and drop to 75 pounds after 60 days. Again these are not hard numbers by any means, but I present them so a person will know that a tremendous weight drop can be expected. As proven by thousands of prisoners of war, such weight loss is survivable.

I finally decided to pack about two pounds of candy per person in my survival kit. That amounted to about 3400 calories for each person. I almost did not pack any food substance at all when I became convinced through research that most people would live the 60 days anyway. Remembering Dr. Bombard's comment about people becoming disheartened and giving up however, I felt that the average person who opened a survival kit, and found no food whatsoever would become quite discouraged. My one motivating factor for including the candy was for morale purposes. If a castaway thinks he is getting some "super duper", high-energy ration, which by the way the candy is, his mental attitude will be lifted.

Once I overcame the food problem for survival, I concentrated next on drinking water. The lack of drinking water kills a large majority of castaways. It seems almost ironic that a person can be surrounded by all that water, yet die of thirst. If I discovered one thing on my own survival expedition, it was to find that starving was not all that unpleasant. However, dehydration was very unpleasant, and that is putting it mildly!

Again I considered Dr. Bombard's comments and experiments with drinking sea water. Dr. Bombard spent a great deal of time experimenting with drinking sea water. He was convinced that humans could drink sea water directly if the body could be adapted slowly to doing so. He was in fact, after many weeks, able to tolerate drinking seawater and maintain relatively normal bodily functions. It is not my place to question Dr. Bombard, but suffice it to say that a considerable amount of research would be required to support advising a castaway to experiment in drinking straight sea water.

Looking for an easy way out of doing a bunch more research, I drove to the Oakland Naval Hospital to ask the doctors just how much water a person needs in order to survive. No one seemed to have the answer. Naval survival books suggest that a quart of water a day is enough for survival. I read accounts of persons in desert survival situations who lost as much as eight gallons of water in perspiration a day hiking in the desert. Dougal Robertson reported that he and his family survived on as little as six to eight ounces of water a day per person for their 36-day ordeal.

The obvious solution to the amount of water needed to sustain life is to take enough water with you to survive for long periods. The problem stems from water taking up so much space, and being so heavy. To pack enough water for a 60-day ocean ordeal would require more space than can be built into any life raft. Adequate water for sixty days of survival would weigh 90 pounds per person, so water for a six-person life raft would weigh 540 pounds, and take more room than the average boat could accommodate. Most general aviation type aircraft would never hold the weight or bulk.

Although the Navy recommends a quart of water a day for a person's survival, I determined from further research that a person can survive on less, and that most castaways reported their ability to trap rain at some point during their ordeal. Rainfall would certainly supplement any water that might be packed in the survival kit.

I need to mention that when I completed the research for my planned experimental expedition, there were only three choices, or methods, for supplying water in a survival kit: (1) to pack sealed containers of water which is still included in many survival kits, but this method takes too much space and the weight is prohibitive. Another problem with containerized water is that once you drink it, you're devoid of it. There is no survival kit today that could hold enough containerized water to support life for an unknown duration; (2) used in some survival kits, including the military's, is a desalinization kit. The chemicals used in desalinization precipitate sodium from salt water. Mixing salt water with the chemicals provides potable drinking water. In retrospect, I compare a drink of desalinized water to a drink from a 55-gallon drum that has been left to rust for years, and stirred up to give a reddish, brown color! The taste alone will make a person throw up. And the desalting kits suffer from the same detractions as containerized water; once used there is no more. The kits are also heavy, expensive, and take lots of space. Each makes about a quart of drinking water. Of course the military is the only organization that can afford the de-salting kits as they are so expensive; (3) the last method for producing drinkable water day after day for long periods, albeit the only one known at the time, was a solar distillation kit. Such kits were used by the military, and were a means of making water day after day for long periods. The kits took about as much space as a de-salting kit, but would produce many quarts of drinking water. The solar distillation kit became the intended backbone of my survival kit by allowing me the means of making water for over 60 days. They could make almost a quart of water on a long, hot day, but much less on a cloudy or overcast day. Being the eternal optimist that I am, I bore the assumption that cloudy days might bring rain.

Today, a far superior method for converting sea water to potable water is the reverse osmosis pump. The pump will make many quarts of fresh water, and is not dependent upon the sun's rays. It does, however, require some body energy, but believe me, even though starving and weak from exhaustion, I would pump this machine to get a drink of water! There were times during my expedition that I would have done almost anything to get a drink. Anyone who goes across an ocean without one of these machines is crazy. That's all there is to it. If I had but one choice of a survival item, I would choose the reverse osmosis machine. One can live many days without food, but only a few days without water.

Meanwhile, I became the world's expert on the operation of the solar still. Living on the water in San Francisco Bay, I performed endless experiments with the solar stills, as I was about to stake my life on its efficiency. I wanted to discover exactly how much water the still made in different types of weather conditions. I spent many boring days playing with it. Sometimes, I would check the water to find it was salty. Discouraged, I discovered that if the still deflated just a little, the freshly produced distilled water became contaminated with salt. A drain cloth at the bottom of the still disintegrated after about 40 days, and became useless. I found that I could repair the cloth by gluing another cloth to the bottom. Finally, I became convinced that the still was reliable enough to stake my life on it.

Decidedly, if a castaway remains very quiet, and rests the majority of the time, the requirement for water decreases. It is equally important for a castaway to conserve what body water he has, as it is to produce water. This brings up clothing. Many castaways die because they are exposed to the sun without cover or clothing. A castaway can lose much body fluid through evaporation, therefore it is extremely important to stay out of the sun if at all possible. If unable to shield one's self from the sun, keep clothing on, and keep clothing wet. Recall Captain Bligh's experience with salt-water drenching.

I should qualify many of the statements in this book by saying that it would take a much greater volume than I am now writing in order to cover each and every aspect of all known survival situations. My book is written primarily to cover ocean survival in temperate parts of the ocean where, perhaps, ninety percent of the population sail or fly. Persons operating boats or aircraft in the very high latitudes of either hemisphere, i.e., outside the temperate zones and above forty degrees north or south, should give special attention to shelter and clothing. One can survive months without food, days without water, but possibly only a few minutes in cold weather.

At my then present stage of development, I felt that the drinking water problem was solved. I told my doctors at the Naval Hospital that I believed I could live on eight ounces of water a day so long as I took care in what I ate, kept my body cool, and stayed out of the sun. The doctors warned that I would probably suffer permanent, or life-threatening kidney failure if I pursued my intent of allowing myself so little water. But my mind was set. I also believed that Mother Nature would provide, but I was to find out differently, the hard way.

During my research period, and especially considering my concern for my kidneys, I searched for the best book on kidneys and kidney function that I could find. That book was one written by Homer Smith, *From Fish to Philosopher*. In this primer for all aspiring kidney specialists, I found a wealth of information. In fact, I discovered a way to increase my water supply by about a third.

It seems that in regards to the osmology or chemical composition of blood in this case, the salts in most ocean water is five times that of the salts in the human blood stream. A biology student will tell you that the water in a cell, submerged in water with five times the salt content will migrate to the body of greater salt concentration. The same process occurs in a swimmer's body. Too long in a pool or ocean, the skin will crinkle from dehydration, denoting the loss of body water. If one should drink straight sea water, water in the blood stream and in the cells will be lost to the sea water, and the body will dehydrate even though the volume of water in the body is greater. It is not that the body does not have water, the problem comes from the fact that the chemical balance or electrolyte balance of the body is thrown off. If the chemical balance of the brain is altered even slightly, a persons ability to function can be life threatening.

The Atlantic which is slightly saltier than the Pacific might be the better body of water to be a castaway in, but the difference is negligible for survival purposes. Again, Dr. Bombard thought's on this were that with enough training, he could tolerate the drinking of sea water to supplement his fresh water. But his suggestion went against everything the Navy taught us. Everybody knows not to drink sea water in a survival situation. But the fact remains, that one can drink sea water. Let me tell you more.

Using Dr. Bombard's research, and the information in Homer Smith's book, I determined that if I were to mix about three ounces of sea water with ten ounces of freshly distilled water, it would effectively increase my water supply, and not draw water from my body. This was good news. Now for the bad.

Sea water has about the same chemical property as Epsom Salts, a well-known laxative. The last ailment a castaway wants is diarrhea. The loss of body water can be so great as to put the castaway's life in jeopardy in a very short time. But the fact remains, if one is tolerant of sea water, one can benefit from drinking it.

There is another aspect to drinking sea water that I might mention. First, the minerals in the water are beneficial; additionally, the minerals in sea water add to its thirst-quenching qualities.

Thor Heyerdahl mentions this, and although I did not make a written note of it, I remembered his observation when I read Homer Smith's book. Heyerdahl had barrels of fresh water on, "Kon Tiki," but he often noticed that drinking the pure water from the barrels did not seem to quench the feeling of thirst in the throat. But, he found that by adding sea water to the fresh water, the feeling of thirst was quenched. Apparently the minerals in sea water satisfy a bodily need.

I never thought during my expedition that I had a problem by adding sea water to my drinking water. A couple of times I even drank straight sea water, and suffered no ill effects. At times, I couldn't tell the difference between sea water and fresh water. I once heard that some parts of the ocean contain great fountains of fresh water that poured out from the sea floor. If that is true, then I must have been over one of those pools at times. I can remember vividly drinking straight sea water that tasted like a cool drink from a mountain stream.

So it is established that most castaways might benefit from a small amount of sea water, but always should remain aware of what their bodies are saying. Toleration of sea water may not be for everyone. A ratio of three ounces of sea water to ten ounces of fresh water may not be tolerable to some people, but a quarter, or half-ounce, of sea water to ten ounces of fresh water could do one a lot of good.

There is a misconception among many people that sea water can be taken through enemas. If sea water is taken in through the rectum, it does not alter the fact that the water is still five times as salty as that in the blood stream, and will cause major dehydration. The same is true of drinking urine. The kidneys operate near maximum efficiency, and the urine that is expelled is going to do nothing to increase life expectancy.

There is a case to be made for taking water through enemas though. Many times a castaway will encounter a rain. The largest rain catchment available is the life raft itself. Much fresh water can be captured in the bottom of a life raft. Even if the raft has sea water in the bottom, that water may be diluted to a safe level, and be drinkable. Unfortunately, there is likely to be all other manner of distasteful matter in the bottom of the raft in addition to sea water. Some castaways found that even though they could not drink the residue in the bottom that collects during a rain for fear of vomiting, they could take the water through an enema. If you are dying from dehydration, it's certainly worth a try, besides it has been tried, and with success. I packed soft plastic tubing in the survival kit for just such circumstances.

There are other ways of obtaining water or liquid to be considered. I, personally, could not, and did not, do the following for fear of becoming ill, but many castaways have. The spinal fluid, and fluid in the eyeballs of fish, birds, and turtles has very little sodium, and will benefit the person who is able to extract and drink the water from these creatures. I equate the sucking on eyeballs with eating raw oysters, some can do it, and some can't. I'm in the latter category.

Blood from fish, birds, and turtles can also help increase the liquid needs, while at the same time, provide valuable nourishment. I hoped that on my crossing, I would just get a lot of rain.

I mention here, my "crossing" because at some point during my research, I began to get an idea about testing out my theories in a real-life environment. First of all, I was intent on building the best survival kit that had ever been on the market, and I began to realize that without a test, how could I be assured that it will be the best kit? And secondly, I began to realize that I would have to do something to promote the kit. My kit was going to be far more expensive than those of my competitors, and I had no money to buy advertising.

It wasn't very hard to determine a "test bed." I was in California, and just over two-thousand miles downwind, and to the west, was Hawaii. The two-thousand miles was as far as any open ocean trip I had ever plotted in my research, and it would take just about sixty days to get there in a rubber raft, or boat.

All of this planning began during the summer of 1973, and I had only been married six months! I knew Judi would understand what I wanted to do, and she would not object so long as she felt I had done everything possible to do it safely.

I don't actually remember exactly how I brought up the subject, but I think I eased into it slowly. I told her about Dr. Bombard's trip, about how it would cost so much to market the kit, that I would need some sort of publicity stunt, and that I would be wasting my time if I didn't do something to get attention for the kit's potential. Also, I told her that the kit really needed to be tested. I couldn't sell something that I was touting as the best survival kit in the world unless I actually knew that it was the best, and the only way to find that out was to give it a real-life test. The seed was planted, and it germinated in my head as I pushed on with the research.

I felt that I had solved the food and water problems. Now I had to figure out how to provide a system of navigation so that a castaway could navigate his life raft to landfall, or at least into a major shipping lane. Although I had received a good deal of training in navigation as a pilot, most of it was in electronic navigation. I knew very little about celestial navigation, but I did know where the experts were. After all, I was in the Navy, and lived next to the Naval Air Station where not only was situated the USS Hancock, my carrier in Vietnam, but also the USS Enterprise. I assumed that I would simply ask the navigators on those ships what they would recommend, and my problems would be solved. Not so.

I went aboard both carriers, and explained to the navigators why I was looking for a system of navigation that was simple, inexpensive, and small enough to be packed in a small space. They suggested a small sextant as the best item to pack.

I was disappointed, and felt there must be other ways. Besides, sextants are expensive, require instructions on how to use them, and on how to use reduction tables that needed to be included with them. At the time, there were no portable GPS (Global Positioning System) units. Even if there had been, the cost would have been prohibitive for packing into a survival kit. I had to keep a lid on cost, or no one would buy my kit.

The problem with selling a survival kit is in trying to sell somebody something they hope they never have to use, and my kit was going to be expensive.

I went back to the library, this time to study navigation. I read book after book on navigation. I studied the Pacific Islanders and their methods of navigation. I studied methods used by early European explorers in navigating the open ocean. What I eventually decided upon was a combination of a lot of navigational techniques.

There were particular parameters in a navigational system that I thought mandatory. First, the navigation system had to be simple. The use of a sextant and reduction tables were far too complicated for the average castaway if they had no previous knowledge of navigation. In fact, that so named "average" person has little to no knowledge of navigation principles. Moreover, in a disaster at sea, the navigator of the boat may be the person who perhaps did not survive the calamity that sank the boat, and someone totally unfamiliar with navigation might have to navigate the life raft.

At last I found a solution in a nomogram which is a mathematical term which describes a graph that could be used to solve a problem, in this case a navigational problem. The nomogram was simple and easy to use and was accurate within about thirty miles of latitude.

Prior to the invention of the chronometer, sailing a parallel of latitude was the standard navigational practice of ancient sailors and explorers. The captain of a vessel would simply sail his craft north or south until the sun, moon, or stars were at their decreed location in the sky for the particular time of year. He would then turn his vessel east or west to maintain the chosen celestial bodies in their relative positions in the sky.

The North Star was important to the ancient navigators because it remains in a very stable position in the sky, and it is located almost over the North Pole. Anyone who has ever used a protractor in school can visualize the technique used by ancient sailors for sailing a parallel of latitude. For instance, if you were in either Hanoi, Vietnam or Maui, Hawaii which are both near 21 degrees of north latitude and sighted across the straight edge of the protractor to the North Star and had a string with a weight on it, that string would cross the protractor at 21 degrees. Now all you would need to do to get from Hanoi to Maui would be to keep your vessel at a position so that the North Star was always at 21 degrees. If you found one day that the string crossed at 30 degrees that would mean that you had moved north and the North Star would appear higher in the sky. You then would have to steer south so that the North Star would appear to settle in the sky until it read 21 degrees again. If you keep the North Star at 21 degrees and sailed east and west you would always hit Maui and Hanoi. That's all there is to it.

As ancient sailors sailed east and west along a selected course, called, "sailing a parallel of latitude," they would try to keep certain stars in the same relative position above them. They knew to make adjustments for the seasons of the year, adjustments that would then assure them of making landfall exactly where they had planned. In order to remember the difference between latitude and longitude, I envision latitude as a ladder set against a globe, South Pole to North Pole, with each rung of the ladder representing a parallel of latitude.

There are a couple of good reasons why ancient sailors sailed parallels of latitude. First, most bodies of land in the world are oriented or stretch from north to south. It would be impossible to sail east or west anywhere in the world and not hit land, except in some very high southern latitudes. So sailing a parallel of latitude is important. With my adaptation of the nomogram, which I later call the, "Solargram," a person with little navigational experience can determine a position of latitude. In fact, in the many survival courses that I've taught, I guarantee that I am able to teach anybody how to find latitude in about 30 minutes. This was my pledge to people who knew absolutely nothing about navigation.

My Solargram will enable a castaway to stay on a parallel of latitude, and with some selected charts, he can determine the latitude of the nearest probable land. I say, "probable" for good reason, and I will discuss this later. If the castaway was not already on exactly the same latitude as his destination indicated by the Solargram, highly improbable, he would have to sail north or south until the Solargram indicated that he is on the same latitude as his landfall destination. For instance, on my expedition, I sailed out of San Francisco, which is about 37 degrees north latitude, and I was aiming for Maui, which is about 21 degrees north latitude. All I had to do was sail south until the Solargram showed that I had intercepted my preselected latitude of 21 degrees north. Then I turned west along that parallel of latitude directly toward Hawaii.

If the castaway happens to have an accurate wrist watch, any one of the new digitals that cost about $25.00, he will have the added ability to compute longitude, or how far east or west his position is along a line of latitude. It is a certainty, that with the Solargram, a castaway can make landfall, and with the added ability to determine longitude with his watch, he could possibly sail a more direct route, plus determine the time it will take to arrive at his destination. With the Solargram, and with an accurate watch, the castaway can determine his exact position almost anywhere in the world to within about 30 miles, a feat which I think is certainly good enough for life raft navigation. On my trip having an accurate watch was nice as a morale factor in knowing how fast I was moving west.

There was one other navigational item that needed to be packed into the survival kit, and that was a chart of the world's oceans. I decided to pack into the Sig II Survival Kit, a set of pilot charts that not only cover all the oceans of the world, but show major shipping lanes, latitude and longitude of land masses, and prevailing ocean currents.

With the Solargram and charts, I formed a navigation system that is simple, requires no prior knowledge of navigation, and is inexpensive.

I was satisfied that I now had solved the food, water, and navigation problems. Next, I turned my attention to the needs of the castaway in the matter of life raft, dinghy, or lifeboat.

During my research I began to consider the type of flotation or raft a yacht might have aboard that would do as a vessel for my voyage across the Pacific. At the time, there was no company that produced or sold a life raft that could be sailed and maneuvered with success. Nor has any company, since I began my expedition of over 25 years ago up to the present writing of this book, produced a life raft that could be sailed.

On my expedition I wished to simulate a castaway's plight as closely as possible. It is fair to say, that most world sailors and pilots take inflatable boats or life rafts for emergencies. I approached every company that produced an "inflatable" that might be adapted for sailing, and asked that they sponsor one of their products for my planned expedition from San Francisco to Hawaii.

It was awkward for me to ask for help. Most people looked at me as if I were crazy. There was just no good way to tell a company president that I was going to sail across an ocean in their inflatable boat with nothing but a survival kit. I was more than embarrassed for I've always been independent and hesitate to ask for help. But my project was becoming more and more expensive, and my part-time job with the Naval Reserve was not going to pay enough to cover everything I needed. I hated to approach people with such a strange request, and more possibly hated their strange reactions. But plod on I did.

There was only one company that showed any interest at all, and that was, Zodiac. Zodiac had been building inflatable boats and rafts for years, and I knew their products to be of high quality. They wanted all the details of my trip, and requested references. As I look back, I think they really would liked me to have submitted to a psychiatric evaluation. However, they did contacted the skipper of my reserve squadron. He was aware of my work in preparation for the expedition, and called to tell me that Zodiac had contacted him, and he told them that I was a stable officer, and that the U.S. Navy had enough confidence in me to have entrusted me with multi-million dollar aircraft along with the lives of my crews.

That must have convinced Zodiac that I was not a total nut case, so they had their North American representative contact me to ask what kind of inflatable interested me. I needed an inflatable that could be rigged with a sail, and maneuvered I told him. No life raft, commercially available, met this criteria. The only inflatables that could be rigged with a sail and maneuvered were the inflatable boats and dinghies. Almost all life rafts were, and still are, round in shape. Unfortunately, it is impossible to sail or maneuver a round inflatable.

I gratefully advised Zodiac that any one of their inflatable boats would be acceptable. Zodiac said they were interested in helping, and that they would consider sending me, free of charge, a Zodiac Mark III boat which was fifteen and a half feet long, and about six feet wide.

I was elated! This was really the first positive step of the entire project. Here was a company that was willing to donate a two-thousand-dollar, "inflatable" to my project! Now, I had to put up or shut up.

All the pieces were falling into place for the expedition to take place. I had been working on the survival kit research for almost four months. It was now November 1973, and I had to set a date on which to depart. My destination was already established, but I had not given thought to when I would leave. I still had an obligation to the Reserves for two weeks of active duty in addition to all the other flying I did for them. Once I departed, there would be no income. Judi relieved the pressure when she took a part-time position at a law office in Oakland that eventually turned into a full-time position.

The Navy squadron to which I belonged was due for carrier qualifications, and there was going to be a carrier available on the East Coast in January. Working on carrier qualification, and going to the East Coast would fulfill my two weeks' active duty obligation. My squadron commander had already told me that I could have time during the summer for my expedition if I were still serious about it.

The Zodiac was not to be delivered until March. I decided that the best time for me to be gone was during the summer months. That would give me plenty of time to decide on how to rig the Zodiac and test sail her. I still had a lot of work to do in locating and assembling the items that would make up my survival kit. Finally, I set the tentative departure month as July 1974. The trip was going to take about 60 days, which would give me the entire summer to cross the Pacific. Once I set the date of departure the trip across the ocean became a reality to me. I was going to cross an ocean in an inflatable boat with just a survival kit to keep me alive. I had done a lot of research, and I was confident that I could do this.

Courageous as she looked on her very first test sail in the Oakland Estuary. Jack London Square is in the background.

We had to hold the helm in large following seas in order to keep Courageous from broaching. We overturned the second day out when a rogue wave that towered above Courageous pitched-poled us.

The two round ball are the water making solar stills. We had to keep the solar stills fully inflated in order to make fresh water. We departed with no water as we planned to make all our water with the stills and we thought we would get some rain. George is inflating the still as they tended to deflate at night as the temperature dropped. The helm is tied off so we do not expend energy steering.

George is having his noon drink. Starving was not physically painful, but being dehydrated was extremely uncomfortable. The "Hawaiian Sling" spear we used to kill the fish can be seen to the right.

Charlie holding the log book. We kept a record of our thoughts, sightings of birds and fish, recipes, and physical condition. We sat under the tarp to keep as cool as possible. We were both still navy pilots and wore the sunglasses to prevent any possible eye damage.

Courageous becalmed. It was a blessing in that we got to rest and dry out, but we made little progress west. This picture was taken 900 miles at sea. The ocean was like a big swimming pool.

Charlie in one of the one-person life rafts. I felt like I was watching a space walk when Charlie ventured out in the little raft. If the wind had come up and he drifted off, he could never have caught up with Courageous.

Charlie lost his wool hat so he had to wear a sailor's hat after the second day. This picture epitomized what we did 99% of the time: just sat and rested. We had to conserve energy as we only consumed a total of six pounds of food in 56 days at sea.

George with zinc oxide on his nose. The doctors were interested in some close-ups so we took these silly looking pictures. We never got so much as a cold on the trip.

George with movie camera. We took some movies; the best of which was the Great White shark swimming around Courageous eating George's tennis shoes.

Charlie taking George's blood pressure. Our blood pressure dropped from a normal 120/80 to 60/0. We could not get a diastolic pressure which did cause us some concerns about our kidney functions.

George talking on the VHF radio to a Braniff Boeing 747 that we saw fly directly over us. We were able to report our position three times during the crossing.

Throw out the life-line across the dark wave,
There is a brother whom someone should save,
Throw out the life-line, throw out the life-line,
Someone is sinking to-day.
—Edward Smith Ufford

III

The Survival Kit

At the heart of organizing a successful survival kit, I would have to include the means to produce water. The solar still that I've mentioned previously met that demand. All I had to do at this stage was find some solar still kits. A large problem loomed because no one manufactured them anymore. However, some units of the military continued to use them, and had surplus stills for sale. The solar stills first came about during WWII when thousands were built. Then the military decided, in the early 1970's, that they could pick up a downed pilot anywhere in the world within 24 hours. Thus, a long-term item such as the still was no longer needed, and the still began to appear on the surplus market.

The solar stills that had been packed in military life rafts were removed, destroyed, or sold for surplus. If I was to develop a survival kit, and risk my life in testing it, I wanted to make sure that solar stills would be available in order to outfit my kits when I returned from a successful expedition.

I began to contact every military surplus station to find out if their solar stills were coming up for bid. I called the military manufacturer of the stills to inquire about buying the patterns and rights to build the stills myself. If I placed an order for fifty thousand dollars worth of solar stills, they would build them for me at $150 per copy. Boy! Was this survival kit getting expensive! But, expensive or inexpensive, it didn't matter either way since I didn't have the fifty thousand to place an order.

Eventually, I purchased almost every available military surplus solar still for an average cost of $2.00 per unit. The A-3 Skywarrior that I flew for the Reserves, took on a new name, the A-3 "Skyvan." All my training flights in the Skywarrior were made to destinations where surplus auctions were held. It was, "bending the rules" to use a Navy plane to conduct my own business, but I accumulated many hours in required training by flying all over the United States. I bent the hell out of the rules in Vietnam to do what Uncle Sam wanted done, so I didn't feel too badly.

I acquired thousands of surplus stills in this manner. Some of the stills were in bad condition, but most were just like new, having no shelf life. In fact, in my tests with the solar stills on San Francisco Bay, I used stills that were over 20 years old.

Today, reverse osmosis pumps for desalinization are available, but that technology was not available in 1974. I spent hundreds of hours testing the solar stills. I wanted to be sure they would make enough water for survival. Luckily, I lived on the water, so I it was easy for me to test the stills. I had to run out to check the water and inflation of the stills about every 15 minutes. It was boring, tiring work, but it was necessary in order to assure myself that the still was going to work, and would aid in the development and recordation of which remedial steps to take if it didn't work. After all, my life was going to depend on those solar stills.

The Sig II survival kit began to evolve. Early on it became clear that any good survival kit needed to be packaged in such a way that water and sunlight would not affect its contents. The largest space in the survival kit was going to be taken up with the solar still so I had to design a container large enough for the still to fit inside. Then the kit itself had to be sized to pack easily into an average sized life raft. I accomplished this by measuring the average size of most life rafts, and then allowed for an average container space. Even though the survival kit really belonged in a raft's container, I had to make the kit a "stand alone" item so that if it were not packed in a raft, or a dinghy, it could be packed on the deck of a boat, and be strong enough to take all the punishment that could entail.

If I packed the kit in a hard container so that it could be stored on the deck of a boat, it would have to be strong enough to bear the weight of a person sitting or standing on it, yet protect the contents from damage. But, once again, the costs to develop such a container approached the outer edges of my budget without a thought yet to the consumer's pocketbook. With some searching and experimentation, I designed a nylon-impregnated, double-walled, water-proof bag. The bag even had one advantage over the hard container, it would conform more easily to spaces within the life raft.

I contracted with a local company to build the bags. The contents would be packed into an inner water-proof bag, then that bag would be packed into a thick, rubberized, nylon bag. The kit, when packed, had to meet one other requirement: it had to float when fully packed. Once I gathered all the contents that would be packed into the kit, I made sure that the kit would float. There were far too many accounts of castaways in their haste to abandon ship having to throw survival equipment into the ocean only to see it sink. To overcome my concern about the chances of damage to the contents should they be stepped on, sat upon, or dropped, I packed all items vulnerable to damage into heavy, water-proof, plastic containers.

Because it was impractical to pack a survival kit with enough food to provide a well-balanced food supply, I decided to go ahead and pack the candy. With the history of many castaways catching fish, turtles and birds, I resolved to provide the unfortunate person with the very best means possible for catching any kind of food that presented itself.

Once again I looked to the library for solutions. I had to find out what kind of sea life a castaway might encounter, and the best way to catch whatever that sea life might be. Over and over again I read castaways' accounts of an abundance of fish swimming around their life rafts, and of their inability to catch them with hook and line. What they needed was a gaff, or spear. Fish are often attracted to shade on the surface of the water such that a life raft would make, and small fish will often gather under a raft to feed on the growth that forms quickly on its underside. The small fish attract larger fish, and so on, until sometimes those larger fish are too large, a peril I was to encounter later.

It was easy to find both a high quality fishing gaff, and fishing spear, either one to prove very effective. Whatever implement I was to select for the kit, I always kept in mind that it should fulfill more than one function, and offer the most benefit, for the person using it. As an example, and because of the disconcerting experiences that many castaways endured with sharks and other large fish, I ordered a spear built strong enough for use as a weapon as well as for snagging food.

Surviving castaways complained of the types of survival knives packed into their life rafts. It was truly a joke. Most of the knives packed into rafts would not even cut an apple. Some were made from metals that would rust away when exposed to saltwater; other knives had no pointed ends with the intention of course, to prevent the castaway from puncturing his raft. Evidence from my research showed, however, that castaways were unanimous in cursing the blunt-ended knives. They prayed for a sharp, pointed-end knife to cut through turtles and fish, and strong enough to use as a weapon when necessary. With clear conscience then, I decided that it was not my function or responsibility to protect the castaway from his own stupidity. If he were not careful with the knife, he would suffer the consequences. The majority ruled. As a result of these well-known requirements, I decided to pack into my survival kit, a SCUBA knife with not only a sharp point, but a serrated cutting edge in addition to a normal, sharp edge. As a sailor, I had had too many bad experiences with the Navy's pot-iron strip of metal packed as a survival knife that rusted almost before one's eyes. The SCUBA knife that I packed was stainless steel, and was large enough to be used as a weapon if necessary.

There were, according to survivor tales, life rafts packed with, "fishing gear", but such "gear" was instead, cheap hooks that rusted in salt water, and lines, more suited for survival in a backyard pond rather than the ocean. There are surviving castaways who claim they caught fish only to have the fish bite through the line and escape. What a frustration! To be sure, such loss could well be overcome by using steel-leadered line. Consequently, I packed 250-pound test steel leader just in case a castaway would have the stroke of luck to catch a really large fish. I also made absolutely sure that the hooks were of stainless steel. I can't tell you how many life rafts I've inspected to find nothing but a mound of rust from what used to be fishing hooks. Amazingly, it seems that most life raft manufacturers cannot conceive of their equipment being used in or near salt water. Or else they're projecting recovery of those lost-at-sea on the short end of the curve rather than planning for the longer range of, say, 60 days, a duration time which I came to view as humanly possible.

If a castaway is given a hook and line with which to fish, then certainly he ought to have something for bait. I packed rubber worms and silver spinners to make the fishing kit well thought-out and effective though not elaborate.

Next, any good survival kit needs a medical kit. Most survival kits contain merely some Band-Aids, tape, and gauze. Educating myself further with a few books on first-aid, I came to the conclusion that the first-aid kit for ocean survival can be kept simple if the right equipment is packed. The truth is, unhappily, that not all contingencies can possibly be covered due to lack of space. Common injuries most often mentioned are cuts and salt water sores. I discovered, after getting cut on my own expedition, that those seemingly small cuts are not so minor after all. They can develop into life-threatening problems if not treated in some manner. Living in a life raft is just plain miserable! It is sorely impossible to keep anything dry. Even in a relatively calm sea, waves break or splash up against the raft, and water or spray enters the raft. It doesn't take long for that water to collect in the bottom of the raft, and create a slimy, stinking mess. Sitting, or living, in that slime causes a number of medical problems for the disadvantaged seaman. Cuts and abrasions turn into exposed infections that develop just by living in the unhealthy conditions that exist in the life raft itself. The smallest cut, if infected, can be so painful that it sometimes makes rest beyond hopeless.

I learned firsthand during my expedition, that cuts and sores do not heal very quickly in the open ocean. Small cuts, to which I would not normally give attention, became at sea, monumental problems because they would not heal properly. First, they swell then become infected. The pain from those cuts surprised me. From thereon, anytime something accidentally rubbed against even a small sore, I almost jumped out of my skin. "Sensitive" does not begin to describe the sensation, nor the pain. It is now easier for me to understand why the castaways who complained of salt water sores, also complained of sleeplessness. The inability to rest results from even small sores.

Salt water sores arise from those small skin irritations. Bacteria enters into the unprotected, exposed areas causing redness, swelling, and sensitivity. Contrary to the known healing effect of salt water on small cuts as we play in the surf, there is a much different environment in a life raft. There, a disgusting profusion of bacteria floats in the scum that forms in the bottom of the boat. The castaway's body is constantly rubbing against the raft as the latter shifts and moves with each little wave. Like bedsores, the chafing soon causes a break in the skin, then the bacteria invade.

Many castaways have died as a result of salt water sores, cuts and burns that would be nothing but minor problems on land. During my expedition, my feet suffered cuts when we overturned in a storm. Eventually, I had to take off my underwear to wrap around my feet so that nothing would rub against the open sores. While the body tries to fight infection, the painful sores work against the body's effort to get the rest needed to fight the infection. The lack of rest is what I deem the most dangerous result of life raft injuries. With deprivation to body and spirit, the body just does not have the energy to fight off infection.

My Navy doctors gave me their professional help on items to pack for combatting infection. Most importantly, the injured area must be kept clean. As sometimes happens in simple matters that become complicated, the solution is simple, soap. The doctors told me that cleansing the affected area with soap and water would go a long way toward the control of infection. Stocking the kit with soap was no problem. I asked the doctors if sea water was okay for washing. In their opinion it presents no problem. I eventually packed my kit with a product called, Betadine, an anti-bacterial washing agent. Betadine is used as a scrub in hospital operating rooms, comes in liquid form, and is easy to pack. I would remember to put Betadine as first on the list of items in my first-aid kit.

Further contributing to the misery of life in a raft at sea is seasickness. It doesn't seem to matter how seasoned, or "salty" a person may have been on his parent vessel, the new motion of a rolling, tossing life raft can defy the stomach of the strongest old "sea salt." It shouldn't be necessary to describe seasickness to anyone who has ever had motion sickness, or airsickness. They are all equally bad. The old Navy saying goes like this: "At first you're afraid you're going to die, and then you're afraid you won't die!"

The most dangerous consequence of seasickness is dehydration. Vomiting causes a loss of so much body fluid, that dehydration is going to be one of the castaway's most compelling problems. If a castaway is losing body fluid from throwing up, and cannot keep water down, he is going to be in severe danger of dehydration very quickly. Therefore, I packed fresh drinking water, and anti-motion pills into the kit in order that the castaway might take the pills before becoming seasick. The best results would ensue of course, if the castaway has the presence of mind to take the pills before getting into the raft, a matter which would take a cool head indeed.

I tried to cover as many contingencies as possible to insure that a castaway would have some kind of medication and dressings to treat injuries of the kind noted by people who were forced to abandon ship. Oftentimes people were cut badly, but had no way to properly secure a skin tear because of this serious omission in first-aid kits. In my opinion, a concerned effort to educate a sailor with some "on the job training" could result in giving him the knowledge in how to treat a wound in lieu of his bleeding to death. With his preventable demise in mind, I packed pre-threaded sutures in the first-aid kit. It's a given that most people have little or no training in how to properly suture a wound, but, based on my own average-type skills, it seemed to me that a desperate person would have the ability to use a needle and thread to sew his own skin in a life threatening emergency. Sewing skin is not a lot different from sewing other heavy material.

I wanted to pack some prescription painkillers, but the idea became one of complication and expense. I do suggest that persons who are going offshore get a prescription for some heavy-duty painkillers just in case they have to set a bone, or suture a wound. One additional item that a person might pack into his own survival kit is his prescription medicine that he takes on a regular basis, i.e., insulin if he is diabetic. For such reasons, life rafts need to be inspected routinely. If a pilot or a sailor were to take his medicine to the raft packer, the packer will pack the medicine inside the raft.

If a person uses eye glasses, a spare pair needs to be in the life raft or survival kit.

When I first started researching the types of survival kits available on the then current market, I was seldom without surprise, as I've said before. Most times that I went to a marine store to inquire about survival kits, the salesman would usher me to the aisle where displayed were flares, whistles, and emergency locator beacons. While these items may be important, I consider them rescue items, not survival items. A castaway cannot eat nor drink a flare. Such items are only handy when a potential rescuer is nearby. Then, flares, whistles, pistols, shouts, or even waving a shirt may catch the eye or ear of a passing rescuer.

There were not many kits that would actually support life for much longer than a castaway could expect to live without the equipment. Some kits contained dried food products, and products high in protein. The latter, I mentioned, take more water for digestion and elimination than other food groups. To be honest, most survival kits were gimmicks. A sailor who spends his money on such gimmicks derives a false sense of security by believing that he is protected in the way of necessities for survival. So many people have died believing in that junk. I often wished I could put the manufacturers of that kind of crap in a life raft, and let them try and survive on what the sell. I've found that even the conscientious person who is trying to pack a good survival kit has no idea of the fundamentals needed to sustain life in a life raft on the open ocean.

With all that having been said as preview, I eventually packed flares in my survival kit. But, they were not the usual products found in most marine or aviation stores. In the Navy, we carried a 38-caliber flare gun that would shoot a flare 600 to 800 feet into the air. Most flares available to the public could not be launched into the air, and burned at relatively low candle power. The truth is, a lone person on the surface of the ocean holding a 500-candle power flare, can only hope to be seen. More likely, he will be disappointed. I can't begin to enumerate the number of castaways who reported lighting their flares when they saw ships or airplanes, but who were passed by, never seen. How discouraging that has to be.

While 38-caliber flares could sub as make-shift weapons, they don't have much "punch," but can certainly scare off a large shark or whale. They burn with tremendous heat. Unfortunately, as good as those flares are, they are simply ineffective during the day. On a bright day, a castaway is competing with a sun that burns at ten-million more candle power. The very best parachute flares burn at fifty-thousand candle power, pale against full sun light. On the open ocean with its white caps, reflections, clouds, and sun, a rescuer might spot a fifty-thousand candle power flare. There is no doubt, however, that on a dark night, a fifty-thousand candle power parachute flare is the best bet to be seen by an approaching ship. If within a person's budget, the parachute flare can be the most effective for the money.

Most hand-held surface flares are worthless, except as a morale factor to the castaway on the open ocean. One other factor in the use of a lesser flare, is its failure to prevent collisions at sea as told in a number of accounts. Large vessels have run over castaways in life rafts as well as collide with other, larger craft. Having been on the bridge of some huge naval ships, as well as commercial boats, I've seen that there are not always meticulous watches kept when transiting the ocean. Of course, it's difficult to keep staring out into the ocean hour upon hour. Many large ships maintain nothing more than a radar watch for traffic such as other large ships! You will read more about my experience with a large ship, albeit, an aircraft carrier, later on in my story.

Less I be remiss, I need to mention that in view of the sun's brightness, bright -burning flares should be reserved for use at night. And there are daylight alternatives. There are flares that give off huge clouds of smoke, usually orange, as they burn. The orange smoke contrasts significantly with anything else on the ocean surface, giving the most visibility, and providing the best chance for being spotted in daylight hours.

Several times I demonstrated those flares to my survival classes. The orange clouds are understandably impressive. But it wasn't until I myself was in need of rescue on the open ocean that I discovered that a 15 to 30 mile an hour wind dissipates the orange smoke in mere seconds. If one lights the flare while a rescue vessel is still a mile or more away, the smoke will dissipate in a strong breeze and the rescue vessel will likely not see you.

There is only one device that can compete with the sun, and that is the sun itself. In the Navy, we carried a small, hand-held mirror with an optical aiming device. While aiming the hand-held mirror, a person can direct the light of the sun very accurately toward a potential rescuer. There are many imitations, but only an authentic glass mirror with an aiming devise should be used for a signal mirror. Many simulations are made of polished steel, or even plastic. These are no comparison to the real, glass signal mirror, because they cannot be aimed nor do their surfaces reflect as well as the glass mirrors.

So I packed the signal mirror, the 38-caliber flares, and the orange smoke flare into the survival kit. I couldn't pack the parachute flares because they cost too much. Even though I wouldn't go across an ocean without them, I just couldn't afford to pack them in my kit.

Once before I mentioned that no life raft company produces a raft that can be sailed, and that is a true statement. But if a castaway should happen to abandon ship with either an inflatable, or hard dinghy, there is a way to sail either of them. On this account, I decided that it would be smart on my part to include the wherewithal to rig a sail with the survival kit. I contracted with a manufacturer of military survival equipment to make aluminum, detachable, cork-filled poles that could be used as masts and lug poles to hold a sail. Included with the poles would be a 7 by 5 foot nylon tarpaulin exactly like the one I used to cross the Pacific. The "tarp" would make a good sail, sun protector and because it was bright orange a signal devise.

A Solargram for navigation was already incorporated into the kit as well as pilot charts printed on water-proof paper. These would aid a castaway in determining which body of land lay nearest, or better spoken, which lay in the most favorable direction for sailing considering the prevailing winds. There was a large plastic water bag for storing rain water that might be caught in the tarp. The inner lining of the survival bag could also be used as a water storage bag. A small compass with a magnifying glass was packed for navigation purposes.

I packed a fifty-foot coil of quarter-inch line to use for a number of things such as rigging the sail, fishing, or securing things in the raft. I packed a first-aid book as well as a survival book. Because cold temperatures can be the castaway's greatest threat, I included a space blanket, which is basically a sheet of reinforced aluminum foil. The blanket can wrap around, to cover the body, help prevent wind-chill, reflect body heat, and be used to signal for help. Sun lotion, and lip balm for fighting sunburn were added for further protection of the castaway.

Probably one of the most important items that I packed into the survival kit was a set of raft repair clamps. To repair an inflatable life raft at sea can be an adventure in and of itself. In author Steven Callahan's book, *Adrift*, there is a description of the almost superhuman effort he expended in using the repair kits that came with his life raft. The manufactures of those kind of repair kits should be put to sea in a life raft and experience what Mr. Callahan went through. It wouldn't take them long to improve their products. This is exactly why I wanted to test my kit myself under actual conditions.

Most of the life rafts I studied came with some sort of patching material, either to force into a puncture or to patch the hole much as in patching a bike tire. While testing the application of these various repair kits, my wife and I had some good laughs. Judi, my wife, who knows nothing about life rafts, recognized the absolute silliness in the written instructions for some of the repair kits. There was an instruction in one kit that advised the castaway to deflate the life raft for best results, and to dry the area to be patched in order for the glue to stick. No, I'm not kidding. This bit of information was in the repair kit of one of the world's largest life raft manufacturers.

Take all the repair kits contained in all life rafts and throw them out if they do not include repair clamps. Raft repair clamps allow a mechanical means of sealing a tear or hole in an inflatable boat. The clamps screw shut over a hole, and will maintain their integrity for long periods. Charlie and I used one for a month. Once I installed over twenty repair clamps on a small raft, and it stayed inflated for weeks. It ought to be criminal for a life raft company to omit raft repair clamps.

Once I completed the process of collecting or manufacturing the items I wanted, I had no doubts that I had put together the world's best, albeit the most expensive survival kit. A kit for four persons was going to cost almost $400.00 at the retail level. But, always in my mind lay the original goal to design a kit that would keep a person alive for 60 days, not a kit that was cheap. I was now confident that I had reached my goal.

For courage mounteth with the occasion
— Shakespeare

IV

Preparing the Expedition

As 1973 passed into 1974 I was still deep into finding the right products for the survival kit. I knew what I wanted, it was just a matter of shopping around and finding high quality products. The doctors at the Oakland Naval Hospital took a lively interest in my research as they slowly began to believe I was serious about sailing across the Pacific with just my survival kit. I wondered if they thought I wouldn't make it alive, but they seemed to believe that I was intensely serious about trying.

They made me feel welcome at the hospital, or in their responses to my frequent phone calls asking questions about physiology and other related matters. They patiently "walked me through" their scientific explanations. One day at the hospital, I asked the lab to check my numbers on the ratio of salt water to fresh water mix. Dr. Peter Lee, who became the lead man for me at the hospital, agreed with my calculations, but reminded me that there was the danger of getting diarrhea from drinking sea water. He was also concerned about the lack of a sufficient quantity of daily water, or the mere eight ounces that I planned for water rations. He thought that even if I did manage to live, I would have permanent kidney damage. This bothered me. But I had to accept his concern as a further risk to my expedition. I was convinced that if I remained immobile, ate the right foods, or no foods, kept my body cool, I could live on the eight ounces a day. Of course, I still believed that I would get rain somewhere along the way to Hawaii. It seemed impossible that one could cross the Pacific ocean and not get rain at some point.

I began to do a lot of night flying with the Navy as my days were taken up with all kinds of projects such as finding suppliers, testing solar stills, and more reading in the library. I enjoyed the night "tanker" hops. There is not a more beautiful city than San Francisco, and the Bay area at night. The tanker hops consisted of two A-3's flying out of NAS Alameda in formation across the bay, over the Golden Gate Bridge and up the coast. The aircraft would separate over the ocean and practice rendezvous at 250 knots or about 300 miles an hour. Once joined the aircraft acting as tanker would reel out the refueling hose, and the receiver aircraft would fly under the tanker and plug into the refueling basket.

The trip across the ocean had always been in my mind as a solo venture, but Judi, on the other hand, applied subtle pressure on me to find someone to go along. While I didn't object to that, I just didn't know whom to ask. I had some wild friends in the Navy, but most were married and had jobs. And anyway, how do you ask someone to sail across an ocean in an inflatable boat carrying no water and little food?

Finally, I thought of a couple of friends who might like the adventure part. One was Dave Pinkham, and the other was Charlie Gore. Dave was a little older than I, but we had gone through flight training together. He and I had been stationed at Whidbey Island Naval Air Station near Seattle, and we shared a common interest in sailing. While we were there, I purchased a Columbia twenty-two foot sailboat, and kept the boat near the base. Every free minute I was down on the boat learning how to sail, just enjoying being out on Puget Sound and having a change from flying for a spell.

One afternoon I invited Dave to go on a sail with me to an island where I'd heard there was a good restaurant. Even though the restaurant was on an island and close to the water, it had no dock. I had a small, plastic dinghy with a little two-horse power motor that we could use to get from the sailboat to the beach. Dave and I reached the restaurant about nine o'clock that night. We could see folks sitting in the restaurant watching us while we anchored, and got the dinghy ready. We must have put on a good show for them, and for good cause. The trip to the island had been much slower than we had planned because of the tides, resulting in more time to drink beer. To put it another way, we were both "four sheets to the wind" drunk. I tossed the dinghy over the side. It hit the water upside down. The two-horse motor was hanging underwater, and the prop pointed to the sky. Immediately, perhaps not that fast, I grabbed the dinghy rope and flipped the boat upright. Water poured from all orifices, scrubbing any hope that the motor would start again, ever. After a couple pulls on the rope however, it did start.

Looking up toward the restaurant, I could now see crowds of people gathered at the windows, all watching our show. Somehow, Dave and I made it to the beach, and walked into the restaurant as if nothing had happened. Everybody thanked us for the show. A lumberjack came over to ask me what kind of motor was on our dinghy. When I told him, he said he just wanted to know because he had never seen a motor, once submerged, start up again, and he wanted one of those! I don't remember much about the return trip. It's lost in a fog of the restaurant diners' generosity. They rewarded us amply by keeping the beer flowing to our table for the remainder of the evening.

Dave Pinkham was an adventurer to be sure. I knew he would never quit if things got rough on a sail to Hawaii. However, Dave had a substantial family agricultural business that was his to run. Even though he expressed interest in the trip, he declined.

Charlie Gore was another good friend whom I had grown to really like, and he had the same love of sailing. He and I served in Vietnam at the same time, though on different carriers. He too had lived and trained at NAS Whidbey Island. When I, as a young Lieutenant JG, needed all the money I could earn to pay for my boat and dockage cost, I made a deal with Charlie. He could use my boat anytime he wished for the one-time price of six-hundred dollars, more or less. He considered it a reasonable deal, and so it turned out to be good for both him and me.

Incidentally the deal with Charlie gave me the opportunity to earn the best, "Field Carrier Landing Practice" (FCLP) record that I ever collected. Routinely, a navy pilot garners lots of FCLP's. The ends of selected runways are marked off to simulate carrier decks. We pilots fly around in circles to shoot landings on that improvised deck, day and night, in preparation for landing on a real carrier at sea. Each landing is graded by the Landing Signal Officer (LSO). At the end of the flight, the LSO gathers the pilots for a debriefing and grading. It's akin to hearing your test scores at school read aloud in front of your peers.

One night I had a hot date with a girl I'd met in Anacortes, an adjacent town to Whidbey. I wasn't scheduled to fly that night, although I reminded the scheduling officer that if anyone canceled I would fly. I was what one would call a "gun ho" pilot. I would fly anytime, anywhere.

My outfit had been doing all-night FCLP's, flying from dusk to dawn. The engines were never shut down as ground crews moved in to "hot refuel". Pilots taxied their planes up next to a fuel truck, and while the ground crew refueled, pilots and flight crews rotated, a pressured prelude to carrier operation.

For these FCLP's I'd been flying the A-3, with pilot and one crewman. As this particular night wore on, and after a long dinner, I suggested to my date that we go down to my boat to finish off some wine stashed in the galley. By midnight I felt no pain. This was the very first time that I was so drunk my speech was slurred. But, so was hers, and we were just having a great time when all of a sudden the boat rocked from side to side, and it sounded as if we had hit something. Being tied to the dock made that impossible. Then someone began beating on the cabin hatch, yelling.

"What the hell is going on?" I blurted out as clearly as I could.

"George, George, you've got a flight!" someone yelled.

I opened the hatch to see Charlie and Don Webster, a fellow pilot, looking down at me.

"I don't have a flight tonight! What the hell do you guys want?" I said with some inflection of outrage.

"Listen, you assholes, get the shit out of here and leave us alone!" I said.

"This is no shit!" they said in unison.

"George, Tabor is sick and can't fly. The scheduling officer put you in his seat. You have 45 minutes to get back to base and fly!" Charlie said somewhat convincingly.

Since I was too drunk to make good sense out of the situation, I told them I'd go fly, but that I had a date. Don and Charlie, good friends that they were, assured me they would look after my date. They would even take her out for a midnight sail. I remember thinking what good friends I had who would do all that for me.

I jumped into my Camero, and charged off to the base. I arrived at the squadron, put on my flight gear, and signed out the airplane. Signing out the plane is the process of looking over the log book on the aircraft to see what equipment may or may not be working properly. I met my enlisted crewman, and together we walked toward the waiting jet with its engines running, undergoing a "hot refuel". I was feeling pretty loose, and my enlisted crewman, who was also called out at the last minute, had alcohol on his breath.

"Hinkley, have you been drinking?" I asked.

"Well sir, I was in the club working on my first beer when I got the word," he replied with more balls than a bull. At almost two o'clock in the morning he was working on his first beer? I couldn't say much. I wondered if he could smell my breath. Hinkley and I boarded our A-3, and off we went.

Generally, a night FCLP period is a little stressful with all the effort going into making nice approaches. But that night I was so relaxed that the plane seemed to fly itself. Everything went perfectly. It felt as if the plane were on rails coming in for the, "touch and go's."

When the period was over, we gathered in the readyroom for debriefing.

"SIGLER!" the LSO called out. "You can go. All 4.0's!" 4.0! Perfect! Every landing perfect! What a night!

Charlie and I had a lot of those good times together. When he returned from Vietnam, he enlisted in the Reserves with me, then he moved to nearby Alameda. When Charlie learned of my planned trip, we talked it over, and he actually wanted to go. I knew Charlie, and I knew he wouldn't quit if things got rough. He had a lot of guts. Besides, he was fun to be with.

The time came to ask him to go, and he agreed. It was the best decision I was to make for the trip. Charlie pitched in, and helped with everything. I finished my research, and briefed him on not only the details, but the possible dangers as well. Charlie too, was looking for something to do but he was more interested in the airlines than was I.

The survival kit was finally complete, and I began to call on marine stores in order to get it on the market. The largest marine store at the time was called, "Johnson and Joseph's," located in Jack London Square in Oakland. Cy Lee was the manager. I made an appointment to talk with him about my kit. Cy was also a sailor, and the first business person to take a bonafide interest in both the kit and my proposed trip. Cy suggested that I meet the owner of C.J. Hendry Company, the parent company to Johnson and Joseph's, and the maker of Elliot life rafts. I was really impressed, and cheered by his excitement over my kit.

Cy made an appointment for me to have lunch with Lee Adams, the owner of C.J. Hendry Company. This was heady stuff for me. We met Mr. Adams at an exclusive men's club in the heart of San Francisco. Mr. Adams was in his sixties I guessed, and no doubt a very smart businessman. Cy thought it would be good publicity for Elliot Raft Company if I were to use their product to sail across the ocean. I gathered that he had already told Mr. Adams about my proposed expedition.

However, I discovered Mr. Adams to be a very pompous man. As dinner progressed, it became evident that he merely wanted to meet me because he thought I must be a nut of some kind. I told him about all my research, and that my philosophy of ocean survival is, "save yourself." Mr. Adams claimed to be from the old Merchant Marine school which preached the adage, "never leave the scene of a disaster." I attempted to explain to him that his philosophy was no doubt valid for a merchant vessel since that type vessel most probably had a long-range radio with which to transmit an SOS, and was giving position reports. If a castaway were at least able to transmit an SOS and a position report, and be fortunate enough to receive acknowledgment from the Coast Guard, he should undoubtedly stay put since a search would begin at his last reported position.

With difficulty, I further attempted to explain to Mr. Adams what my research had taught me about recreational sailors who sail their own boats across oceans. Many do not have long-range radios, their boats don't have water-tight bulkheads as do merchant vessels, and they tend to sink so quickly that the possibility of their transmitting an SOS is remote. Mr. Adams' response to my explanation shocked me. Here was a man who owned a company that not only made life rafts for the Merchant Marine world wide, but marketed a version of that raft for the recreational sailor.

As well as I remember, and I remember very clearly, his reply was, "Those damned fools (the recreational sailor) shouldn't be out in the ocean anyway. If they sink, they deserve what they get," meaning I suppose, death. Not only was Mr. Adams not interested in my endeavor, but also against Elliot their taking any part in the project. He said I would never accomplish my goal of sailing a raft across an ocean. This pompous old man who I learned had never been in the water in his own product was telling me that I would never make it! I had a tough time believing that a man who made his living selling life rafts was only interested in the money, and not in saving lives. He considered his customers to be, "damned fools."

Although I didn't sell any survival kits to C.J. Hendry, Cy Lee later purchased ten of my kits for his two stores. As I said, Cy was a sailor. He knew that what I claimed had not only merit, but was plainly the truth. These were my first sales, and I will always remember Cy Lee as a man who really helped me believe in what I was doing. My talk with Mr. Adams, however, taught me that it would be an uphill battle to convince people that my kits were different and better.

More than ever, I was eager to test my kit under realistic conditions. I had to prove my credibility, and the credibility of my kit. A trip of the magnitude I planned would give my company and the survival kit instant recognition and credibility. If there had been enough money for advertising and promotion I may not have taken the raft trip. I don't know to this day. I do know that I had an increasingly strong drive to test the kit. With this thought, I could not shake my strong belief that I could save lives. Never once did I have a conscious doubt about the kit's worthiness. My only doubts lingered on whether or not I had confined the kit to too narrow a philosophy. There were no extras planned for it, only those items described on a castaway's "wish list" to help him stay alive.

At this point, I feel it is important to explain that the kinds of items omitted from the kit were the kinds that many mariners were accustomed to seeing in survival kits and life rafts such as oars, dried or canned meats, blunt-end knives, glue-on patching kits, etc. Many people asked me why I didn't include some kind of game or playing cards, which would give the castaway something to do. Truthfully, to that query I had a selfish reason for objecting. I was terrible at party games, I always lost. The last thing I wanted in my kit was a game that I would lose day after day. Being stuck in a life raft is depressing enough without losing a simple game repeatedly. Besides, a game would drive up the cost, and take up critical space.

I did not pack an emergency radio or ELT because, in 1974, there was not wide-spread reception for ELT's except for land-based units. Further, radios cost a great deal of money. To pack a radio would double the price of the survival kit, and finally, I consider radios and ELT's rescue equipment, not survival equipment. Castaways can't eat or drink a radio. I did recommend that a sailor or pilot carry an ELT, and have it packed where it could be gotten to very easily.

I do believe that anyone who goes out to sea today without an ELT makes a big mistake. If a radio works and someone hears it, you can be saved in a matter of hours. Assuredly, I wouldn't want to spend one more minute at sea in a life raft than is absolutely necessary. In my opinion, a mistake that many people make, and some were my customers who didn't live through their survival experience, is that they purchase emergency radios, flares, and other rescue equipment, leaving little else to spend on critical survival equipment. Today, ELT are inexpensive, and it is easy to see that a sailor might be tempted to buy an ELT before spending hundreds of dollars on a survival osmosis water maker.

I recommend that a sailor or pilot first plan his survival kit as fully as possible, and purchase items that will keep body and soul together. If he has money left over, he might then consider a radio. It is absolutely wrong to buy a radio and a life raft, and think a survival kit is complete. For example, there are numerous and recent accounts of castaways who activated emergency radios until the batteries ran dead. No one heard their calls. Compounding their foolhardiness, they may have run their batteries dry in the many areas of the world not covered by electronic surveillance.

My next few statements on survival are probably some of the most important in this entire book. My survival kit was designed to keep the castaway alive for at least sixty days. I have already quoted the medical fact that without food, most healthy persons can live 40 to 60 days: without water, 8 to 12 days. Unfortunately, many castaways never live beyond the first few hours of their predicament. The reason? The cold. They are exposed to the elements without clothing or some means of keeping warm. When I am asked what the one most important survival item is, I most always say, clothing.

Even in temperate parts of the world where water temperatures range from the lower seventies to upper eighties, the temperature is still ten to twenty degrees below body temperature. Throw in a little wind, a drop in night air temperature, and the exposed body will soon become chilled to the bone. More castaways die from exposure than from all other causes. If a person were faced with the abandonment of his vessel, the second most important item he needs after the life raft, is clothing. Surprising to me is the number of castaways who end up in a life raft dressed in nothing but a swimsuit.

While it wasn't practical to pack clothing into the kit, I did include a space blanket to help the person who might be the one in a swimsuit. A fundamental in physiology is that a person will quickly become hypothermic in very cold water. His body will then cease to function. Usually, when the body core temperature drops to as low as ninety degrees, a person loses his ability to function and think properly. At eighty-five degrees, the person will likely become unconscious. Death is almost certain at eighty degrees. With that being said, there are many accounts of persons who have survived with much lower core temperatures. One such case recently occurred when a mother found her young daughter outside their house on a freezing night. The little girl's body was so cold that it was stiff. The mother rushed the girl to the hospital where she had a recorded temperature of 65 degrees. Amazingly, the little girl was revived and seemed to have suffered very little from the experience.

Because this is a book on survival, I think a story that happened to me can be an important lesson in not giving up. In doing the research for my survival kit I read hundreds of medical journals and thousands of accounts of people surviving in the most extraordinary situations. I once read of a young boy who had drowned in a very cold stream and was under water for almost 45 minutes. That boy was revived and survived with little permanent physical or mental damage. That story stuck with me.

What seems to happen is there is a mechanism in the body that closes down when a person is submerged, especially in cold water. That mechanism slows the body's functions in some sort of protective state that we still do not fully understand. I mention this here because it has to do with water survival and because of an incident that happened to me when I was in the Naval Reserve.

I was the Safety Officer of my A-3 squadron at NAS Alameda. Because I lived close to the base I often went into my office to catch up on work. One Saturday morning I was working in my office at the base when one of the mechanics came to my office and asked me if I knew that an A-3 had just gone into the water.

I was so surprised at the question that I asked where, not suspecting it was NAS Alameda he was talking about. He said that an A-3 had just gone in the water at Alameda. I ran to the Skippers office to see if he knew anything. He said that he was watching the airplane taking off, but the plane aborted the takeoff and ran off the runway into the water. I asked how long ago did this happen, and he replied about 10 minutes ago.

Because I had training as an accident investigator, I asked the Skipper if he wanted to go out to the accident site with me. He declined, but I decided to go see if I could help.

When I arrived at the accident site there were about 30 people standing at the end of the runway not too far from the water's edge. I couldn't see any A-3 so I asked the first person I saw if the airplane had already been towed back to the hangar. He said no that it had sunk. There were no rescue people in the water, although there was a Coast Guard helicopter hovering over the water. I began to sense that something was very wrong. I ran to the water's edge and asked one of the Crash and Rescue people if the crew had gotten out. He said that no one had gotten out of the plane. Because the A-3 community was very small, I realized that it was some of my friends who were in that cockpit, and no one was helping.

One person had a hand held radio and seemed to be in charge. I ran over to him and asked him if he was able to talk to the helicopter. He indicated that he was in contact with the chopper. The plane had gone into the Oakland Estuary which was only a mile from an office I had on the Estuary. I told the person on the radio that I had SCUBA equipment at my office and if the chopper would take me there, I could come back and try and find the pilots. The chopper flew me up to my office. I had a friend who was also a SCUBA diver who had an office next to mine. Fortunately he was working that morning so I told him the situation and asked if he could help. Without hesitation he grabbed his gear, and we stopped by my office where I had a tank of air and a diving mask.

The chopper flew us back, and we jumped out over where we suspected the aircraft was. The water smelled of jet fuel and the visibility was poor, but the estuary was only about 40 feet deep so we didn't have far to dive to get to the bottom. The trouble I had was in the fact that I had no weight belt and no back pack to hold my tank. I had to swim with one hand while holding the tank with the other. I surfaced and took off my uniform, undressing down to my skivvies. Again I dove under. The current was pretty bad making it difficult for me with just the one hand and feet to propel me. I could reach the bottom, but I could find nothing. I couldn't figure how I could fail to find an airplane as big as an A-3. I surfaced to find that the current had taken me away from the area. The other diver was evidently not having the same problems as he had fins, backpack, and weight belt.

I swam back to where I thought I was right over the aircraft only this time I swam up current just a little so that as I dove down the current would take me right into the aircraft. But again all I could see and feel was the muddy bottom. Again I surfaced. When I got to the surface I saw a crewman's body being pulled into the chopper. The chopper flew about 200 feet to the end of the runway where an ambulance was waiting. I saw them drape a blanket over the body without even attempting to revive the crewman. The story of the boy being saved after drowning was vivid in my memory, and I began to yell at the medical people not to give up. I yelled as loud as I could, "Don't give up! He can be revived! Don't give up! Try and revive him!" I could tell that there was absolutely no attempt being made to try and revive the crewman. He had only been in the water about 40 minutes, and the water was cold. In addition to that, he might have been wearing his oxygen mask, which would have worked under water.

I was desperate that they should not just cover the body and take him to the hospital. I swam towards shore and told one of the Crash and Rescue people to tell the medics that they needed to try and revive the crewman. I couldn't go into detail, I just told him that he could be revived. They needed to work on him. The man walked over to the medics, and I assume told them what I said. They took no action and began to close the ambulance door. "Don't give up on him!" I yelled as I swam closer to shore. "He can be revived." The ambulance drove off. No one was in back with the body. They never tried to revive the crewman who turned out to be the navigator, a man I had flown with a number of times. If the medics had read the same medical report on the young boy that I had read, they would not have given up.

When I talked to my friend who had found the navigator, he told me that the navigator had released his seat belt, exited the aircraft through the overhead hatch, inflated his life vest, but was caught by the parachute lanyard. He told me that the navigator must have realized that the lanyard was holding him down, as his survival knife had been pulled out of its holster. So the navigator was not injured in the accident, but died trying to reach the surface which was only 10 feet above him.

It makes me sick to this day to think that the navigator may have been saved if someone had known what I knew. Now you know. As Winston Churchill always said, "Never give up." The Navy medics not only gave up, they never tried. I believe that man would be alive today if someone had at least tried to revive him.

I think the lesson in this accident is one that belongs in this book on survival. If those medics had known what I had just read in the medical journal, they would have tried to save my friend. I felt hopeless standing there in the water watching the ambulance drive away, knowing that through lack of knowledge, the medics had just passed a death sentence on my friend. But now back to my survival story.

Time began to slip by very quickly. Charlie and I were still flying in the Reserves, searching for solar stills, and preparing for the trip. We were becoming very anxious to get the Zodiac. Finally, one day we received a call from the distributor. Our Zodiac had arrived, and we could pick it up.

Charlie and I drove to the distributor together, and they gave us a, "how to" demonstration for inflating and assembling the boat. It was larger, and much heavier than we had anticipated. Running boards fit into its bottom, and there was a wooden transom for mounting an outboard motor. There was a foot pump for inflating the five separate inflation chambers, each chamber designed so that if one or two were punctured, the inflatable would not sink. It took about fifteen minutes for the dealer to unpack and inflate the raft. When Charlie and I tried it for the first time, it took us almost an hour. After that, we didn't practice assembling and disassembling the Zodiac. We planned to keep it in the water at my houseboat, and to begin testing it and the sailing rig on forays out into San Francisco Bay.

On the drive back to Alameda, Charlie and I realized that we had to name the boat, and christen it in proper naval tradition. We purchased a bottle of cheap champagne, and began to think of a name. I don't remember the other names we came up with, but we agreed on the name, *Courageous*. Somewhere in Charlie's past he had read a book or seen the movie, *Captains Courageous*. So that's how we came to be known, we were the "Captains Courageous."

We put the boat together at the marina, and floated it to the dock. It looked a whole lot smaller in the water. Christ, it was like handling an elephant out of the water, yet it looked like a toy boat in the water. I think Judi was a little shocked at its size. It looked so fragile, not like something destined to cross an ocean. I acted real excited about the boat, and showed her all its safety features, especially the fact that it had five separate inflation chambers and really couldn't sink.

Never once did I consider giving up my plan. Perhaps any normal person would have had some periods of doubt, but I don't dwell on negatives. I had established a goal of sailing that boat to Hawaii, and the power of that goal just did not allow for any negative thoughts.

A set of conditions that I imposed upon myself, and to which I intended to firmly hold, was the simulation of an actual castaway's plight in as many respects as would be possible. The inflatable boat was my first requirement. Now I had to rig the boat with gear I considered might be available to the average boater. As it turned out, I was able to buy all of the rigging at Wards Department Store. The sail was the same five by seven foot tarp that was packed in the survival kit. The line that held the mast up, and held the sail was the same line packed in the kit. The mast was made from a piece of wood similar to an oar handle, and the rudder was an oar. At this point in time, I had not yet found a source for a mast pole that could be packed in the survival kit, so I had to assume that a sailor could find something on his yacht to use as a mast and lug pole, i.e., a broken mast, boom, oar, spinnaker pole, etc.

Later I did include in the survival kit, a detachable pole that could be used as a mast.

The rigging on our raft remained very simple. Three lines held up the mast, the rudder was mounted on the wooden stern, and VOILA! she was ready to sail. We added one item to the Zodiac that I borrowed from Dr. Bombard. He equipped his boat with leeboards that enabled him to tack more effectively. So we cut two pieces of plywood, and mounted them on a plank we had already mounted on the inflation tubes. The leeboards took up a great deal of room, and as it turned out, we never used them on the trip to Hawaii. In fact, the reason we mounted the boards was for tacking to a beach when we got to Hawaii instead of ending up on the rocks. If anyone doubted that I intended to make it to Hawaii, they would have thought differently to see that I had even prepared for the landing problems on Hawaii's rugged eastern coast.

We purchased a small six-horse power engine for the Zodiac so that we could more easily take it out in the Bay and beyond for "shake down" cruises. But, we had no plan to keep the engine on the Zodiac for the actual trip across the ocean. The Zodiac did not sail well, but we had expected that. With no keel, it had to be sailed downwind, and we could only change the direction downwind about thirty degrees either side of centerline. This meant that we were committed to sailing with the wind as would any castaway in an inflatable.

Somewhat unexpectedly, we found a problem with the solar stills. The stills were designed to float in the water next to the life raft. But, when they were pulled through the water behind the Zodiac, they tilted over, letting in sea water to contaminate the fresh water. And this was not the biggest problem with the stills; they would self-destruct after a short period of being pulled through the water. The problems we had then are irrelevant now with the advent of reverse osmosis pumps, but suffice it to say, we finally mounted the stills on the Zodiac's inflation tubes where they worked just fine.

I spent a couple of long days in the Zodiac, leaving the houseboat early in the morning, motoring through San Francisco Bay, under the Golden Gate Bridge, and out into the Pacific. I didn't go far out to sea, only a couple of miles, to see how the boat handled in rougher water. It was a peaceful way to pass a day, floating in the boat, waves gently rocking me.

The Zodiac gave a very pleasant ride even in heavier seas.

As I prepared for the trip across the ocean, I began to read more books about ocean sailing. When Charlie and I sailed to Hawaii, neither of us had any experience sailing in the open ocean, except in our Zodiac. We had been stationed aboard aircraft carriers, but had never been on a vessel less than nine-hundred feet long. By reading books on sailing, we hoped to make up for what we lacked in experience. That is the real motivating force for my finally writing this book. One doesn't have to have been a castaway to learn how to survive. Reading this book will help one prepare for survival and appreciate the problems.

Zodiac had more than a passing interest in the success of our trip, and wanted to make sure we received maximum publicity with their boat in the forefront. Zodiac and I made a perfect team. They knew their product would make it to Hawaii, and I knew I would be in it. Admittedly, there were a lot of fine inflatable boats on the market, but Zodiac was the only manufacturer willing to put its reputation on the line. Our Zodiac distributor drew up a press release, and gave the story to all the local newspapers and TV stations. Before too long, we began to receive calls about the trip. The local papers came down to the waterfront to take pictures, and our story and pictures made all the local papers. Perhaps our being navy pilots lent a little credibility to the story that it might not otherwise have had, so at least we weren't painted as a couple of nuts, but described rather as a couple of serious people determined to test our concepts and ideas.

Someone introduced us to the Mayor of Oakland, Mr. Reading, who took us on as his own special project, particularly to make sure the Port of Oakland would reap some benefits from our publicity. He was a great help later when we were ready to depart for the trip.

We were still working with the doctors at the Naval Hospital. The reason why the medical aspects so interested me was that for the first time, we, as "castaways" were to have our medical charts well-documented prior to our departure. Actual castaways had their conditions documented following their ordeal but had no baseline with which to compare their condition prior to their ordeal. With ourselves as guinea pigs, we would keep a day by day record of our physical condition, and chart the deterioration that was bound to occur on the trip. The comparison of our pre-departure condition with our arrival condition would be valuable in assessing the methods needed in helping castaways or downed airmen survive. Our example could provide hope to those who would learn and remember it, or our endeavor could result in developing procedures that are not now known.

The doctors wanted to support us as much as possible, and Dr. Lee began to see an opportunity to do some meaningful research. The Navy's Chief of Staff was contacted through official channels to determine if the Navy would officially support us with their medical research. Although Charlie and I weren't privy to what was happening in the wings, we understood there was interest, but that they didn't believe we would make it alive. Frankly, they believed that we would die at sea, and they didn't want to be involved by giving us their endorsement, particularly because of public relations concerns as well as any legal implications.

The sum of the Navy's interest was in their provision of an old Quonset Hut on the hospital grounds. It hadn't been used for anything but storage since WW II, so it was cleaned up, and a couple of beds installed. The Navy planned to do a full set of base-rate studies on us in order to prepare before-and-after charts—in case we did made it. All of this was strictly unofficial, and we could tell no one that the Navy was even doing these basic studies.

The publicity in the newspapers triggered a movement by the Coast Guard to prevent our expedition. The commander of the local Coast Guard district in San Francisco contacted us with the letter asking us to defend our position as to why we think we should be allowed to go. Basically the letter said that the Coast Guard was not in support of what it considered "manifestly unsafe" voyages, and that they intended to prevent our departing on such a voyage. We were requested to respond to their letter and explain why we thought we should be allowed to go.

This was a real blow to us. We had never thought to ask the Coast Guard for permission to sail across the ocean. Charlie wrote a response to the commander explaining that what we were doing was intended to save lives. After receiving the letter, the Coast Guard said they intend to prevent us from going as they did not think we would be successful, and a rescue at sea would cost the tax payers a great deal of money.

We appreciated the Coast Guard's position, but we did not think they appreciated all the preparation we had put into this project. We figured that all the Coast Guard really knew was what they had read in the papers. On our numerous calls to the Coast Guard, it became evident that they thought we were just seeking publicity for a stunt.

We arranged a meeting with the Commander in charge who had written the letter to us. At that meeting it became clear that he had already made his mind up to deny our going. No matter how well we answered his questions, he gave some lame answer back. He asked about how we intended to make water. We told him all about the solar still and how much water they made and how much we planned to drink per day. He said he had never heard of a solar still. This was almost impossible as he was a Coast Guard pilot and had gone through the same training as a naval pilot. We could not believe he did not know what a solar still was. In fact, he was such an asshole, we figured he was just lying to us. He talked at least 30 minutes about his concern that we have proper navigation lights on the raft and a mast head light. He was also concerned that a vessel crossing the ocean should have an autopilot. It became obvious to us that he had already made us his mind prior to our meeting, and we were wasting our time with him. We had to go over his head in the chain of command and talk to someone who could think.

We got an appointment with the Captain who was in charge of the area. This time we took a survival kit with us and gave a detailed explanation of each item and how it was intended to be used. The Captain was a smart guy and realized that we were not out for a publicity stunt. He agreed to let us go.

A life on the ocean wave,
A home on the rolling deep.
—Epes Sargent

V

Departing for Hawaii

The morning of July 4, 1974 was overcast and foggy with very little wind. I slept well during the night, and woke up early so that I could take care of any last minute details. We were scheduled to meet our mother ship at seven o'clock and depart Jack London Square at eight o'clock. *Courageous* was tied up in her dock next to our houseboat. Charlie and I motored her across the estuary from Alameda to Oakland where there were already some newspaper people on the dock, and television crews were setting up their cameras.

We pulled *Courageous* up to the yacht that was to take us out to the Farallon Islands which are about 30 miles off the Golden Gate Bridge, and with the help of the crew we pulled *Courageous* aboard. I was uneasy about dragging the Zodiac over jagged edges for fear of damaging her before we ever got started, but she suffered no damage and was tied down. I then took the outboard motor back home. We would no longer rely on mechanical power for *Courageous*.

Mayor Redding came out to say good-bye and good luck, and the TV people interviewed us. I was excited but relieved to finally be leaving. I harbored no doubts that we were going to make it to Hawaii. Charlie and I were going to demonstrate that castaways could sail a long way to save themselves if they had the proper survival equipment. We would also prove my Sig II survival kit to be the best on the market.

My sister, Carole, and her husband David, arrived along with some close friends whom we had invited to go with us for farewells at the Farallon Islands. Carole always thought I was a little on the "nutty" side so she bore the event with filial indulgence. Notwithstanding my sister's attitude, most friends, and the business people who came to know us, judged us as more than adventure seekers. They sensed that we, indefatigably, intended to prove our theory that we would save the lives of some future castaways.

As soon as we bade our last dockside farewells, our friends joined us in boarding the yacht for the three-hour trip to the Farallons. The trip was awkward. Friends and family ran an emotional gamut from sadness to elation; while some were sad and crying, others partied. Unable to contain my own excitement, I partied. Charlie spent a good deal of time with Nancy, cuddled up in a corner, and I stayed busy talking with Judi and friends. We had arranged for an enormous onboard feast, and Charlie and I stuffed ourselves. Unfairly, I guess, it was the only thing we did at variance with an actual distress situation, the opportunity to cast off in an inflatable life raft with full stomachs.

The water was benevolently calm that morning, allaying my worries about damage to *Courageous* from rubbing up against the mother ship as we launched her. As we approached the Farallons, I made a trip to the pilothouse to have a chat with the skipper. I asked that we launch the Zodiac downwind of the yacht so as not to be run over by the yacht, nor crushed alongside in the up-and-down swells. Thanking him for the ride, I asked for one more favor, that once we were in the Zodiac, and had pushed off, to "Please depart right away." I felt that it would be hard on Nancy and Judi to watch us for any long period as we sailed southwest-ward, and out of sight in that small raft. In other words, it was bound to be less emotional for everyone if the mother ship turned about as quickly as possible. Everyone gathered on the fantail to help launch *Courageous*. I dropped into the raft first, and held her off the mother ship while Charlie handed across the survival kit, radios, and balance of the gear. I leant over and gave Judi one last kiss, and Charlie said his good-byes to

Nancy as he boarded *Courageous*. We pushed off, and cleared the yacht. The Captain, taking my suggestion, immediately turned about and motored back to San Francisco. I unpacked the movie camera in time to record our departure, and Charlie took some still shots.

The Farallons came into site through the fog. Visibility had improved to about five miles, and we could see the surf breaking against the shore. Seas were still smooth with just a light swell. There was a slight breeze from the northeast, precisely as we had expected.

Only now, years later, will I admit my ambivalence in watching that 60-foot yacht on its way back to land while we, in a 15-foot rubber raft, sailed in the opposite direction toward Hawaii. Charlie and I watched the yacht until it became a small speck on the horizon, then we began the job of hoisting the sail, and getting underway. We'd been in the area off the California coast once before when, on one of our "shake down" trips, we sailed and motored the 90 miles to Monterey, so we felt comfortable in the familiar waters.

Emphasizing once again that neither Charlie nor I had open-ocean sailing experience except for our recent trip to Monterey where we were rarely out of sight of land; we were true greenhorns. Except for all the sailor stories that I researched, I had no inkling of what we were to experience. And Charlie merely had the benefit of my briefings. I hoped we had made up in preparation for what we lacked in experience. We were intent upon simulating the plight of castaways as nearly as possible. However, Charlie and I shared the one experience of having been to sea on aircraft carriers, and shared the advantages of being in excellent physical and mental conditions. We had not had to endure the trauma of evacuating a vessel in distress, nor having had to escape a fire, explosion, or a sinking. Our wits were about us. We were confident and trusting.

We were on our own now, no turning back! Any mistakes from here on could spell disaster for us. The air temperature was in the mid sixties, with a water temperature of 59 degrees. We mounted the radar reflector on top of the mast in case a passing ship bore down on us in the fog or at night. We were right smack dab in the middle of one of the world's busiest shipping lanes, and we didn't want to be run over by a ship on our first night out! There are far too many accounts of sailors in small rafts being run over by merchant vessels.

Once we had all the gear stowed, we each took a Dramamine for insurance against seasickness just as we suggested a castaway do. There was just enough wind to catch the sail, and pull the bow of *Courageous* to a southerly direction. We weren't moving very quickly, but were going in the right direction more or less. The sky was still overcast, and the fog was burning off. Our fears of merchant ships running over us lessened as the fog dispersed.

I mounted the solar still on the aft pontoon, but anticipated next to no water-making with the overcast sky. I began to wish I hadn't eaten quite so much chocolate because I was already getting thirsty.

As I later taught students in my survival classes, a castaway must remain aware at all times of his body temperature as it relates to cooling and heating. I read of people who were stranded in winter survival conditions while wearing so much clothing that they froze to death. The reason being, that while hiking they were unaware that their bodies generated so much heat and moisture. They sweated even though the air temperature was below freezing. The sweat soaked their clothing, and when they stopped to rest, the wet clothing turned to ice which in turn reduced their body temperatures. They had started out with plenty of clothing that would have kept them alive in the freezing temperatures, but they neglected to monitor their bodies. Once they began to sweat, they should have shucked some clothing to maintain steady body temperatures to prevent their clothing from becoming saturated with perspiration. Rule to remember: over-clothed is as bad as under-clothed.

Charlie and I had the opposite problem. We had to make sure that when the temperature rose, we kept our clothing wet with sea water to prevent our bodies' from losing precious water in trying to stay cool. It is as important to conserve what body fluids there are as it is to catch or make water to put into the body. It would be a long time before we would sail far enough south where we could strip down yet not get chilled. The water temperature was 59 degrees, so the lightest of breezes chilled us very quickly there on the surface of that cool water.

As the first day wore on we settled into our watch routine. At four o'clock that afternoon, Charlie took the watch. He would stay on the helm until eight that night. Four hours on, four hours off, was our plan. We hadn't given a thought to tying off the rudder, so the helmsman had to hold the rudder, and steer as close to the wind as possible to give us as much progress west as the wind would allow. We didn't worry about the heading so much as we worried about our being pushed eastward toward the beach. We trimmed the sail until it back-winded, then attempted to steer as southerly as possible. Our initial headings were south-southeasterly, not great for some-one going to Hawaii. However, we knew that the prevailing wind and currents along the California coast were going to take us a long way south before we intercepted the tradewind belt that would help us head west.

It's difficult to describe just how peaceful and serene it is close to the water with only the sound of the waves splashing against the raft, a soft breeze blowing, and the occasional sound of a fog horn announcing someone's entrance to the bay. The ride was a lot quieter without the motor, and less odoriferous without the gas fumes. There was more room, and no smell of oil and gas underneath the tarp where we rested.

We talked a good deal that first day. Charlie had been dat-ing Nancy for a few months, and was thinking about getting married. As an old married man of a year and a half, I con-fided to Charlie that getting married was one of the smarter moves I ever made. I was sick of going to bars to meet women, and not liking the kind of women I found there. I never was too much of a woman chaser, and I think it was because I pre-ferred the outdoor life to bars. I enjoyed sailing on Puget Sound, but didn't meet many girls sailing. I liked to go spelunking, or cave crawling, but heck, not many women in caves either. Since childhood I'd been an outdoor type, and it seemed to me that women didn't do fun things like sailing, camping, cave crawling, flying, etc.

Then I met Judi. Our first date was more or less to a bull-fight, after which we met as often as we could. She was from Vancouver, Canada, and was staying in Rota for a few days, and I was stationed aboard a carrier operating nearby in the Mediterranean Sea. Even though I had to put in flying time, I managed to get off the carrier, and bike back to Rota while she was there. When we compared our travel itineraries, it hap-pened that the carrier was going to be in Trieste, Italy, about the same time that she had planned to be in Yugoslavia. We plotted to meet in Trieste sometime in the next couple of months, but I came very close to missing her. We had planned to meet at the American Express Office in Trieste at a certain time, but the carrier was late arriving. She had waited four hours for me. Finally giving up, she walked away from the office, gave one final look backward, and saw me running toward her. I had finally located the office after several wrong turns in my haste. It was so close. We may never have seen each other again.

Although Charlie and I had been friends for a couple of years, I enjoyed hearing his life story for the first time, and I hoped he enjoyed mine. Finally, Charlie crawled under the tarp, and tried to get some rest. Down there under the tarp, neither one of us could stretch out because the sleeping area was only five feet long, and we are each about six feet tall. We rested mainly in the fetal position, changing positions often because the bottom of the raft was a wooden floor, and our bones hurt if we stayed in one position too long.

Altogether, I thought it was rather nice down there under the tarp. There was less wind noise, it was warmer, and the spray from the waves didn't keep me awake. It was like entering into a little, secure world of one's own. If there was any privacy at all, it was time spent under *Courageous'* tarp. One could be alone with one's thoughts, or a time for reflection so to speak. I'm sure each of us enjoyed our rest periods, and our privacy under the tarp.

We spotted a couple of ships far to the west that were making approaches to the bay area, a sure confirmation that we were far enough east to be out of major shipping lanes. Most of the ships that we saw that day still remained off to our west. The raft was handling nicely, but we found it a trifle tiring to hold the rudder continuously.

When darkness came on that first night out, it was barely imaginable that we would be confined to this raft for over two months. The clouds had broken, and we could see stars blinking through. The lights of the bay area shone clearly on the eastern horizon. We'd been at sea for over six hours, but had not actually gone far. We could no longer see the Farallon Islands, but could see, by the lights on the horizon, that we had not covered more than ten miles to the south.

Then the wind began to pick up. It began to blow a steady ten knots, and *Courageous* made considerably better time than she had the previous few hours. The waves pushed us along too, although they were not more than three or four feet high. *Courageous* rode them easily. At eight that night, I took the helm. Inasmuch as sailing directions went, passing the watch on to the next person was easy. Charlie instructed me to steer as far west as I could until the sail backwinded. It didn't matter what our heading was so long as we tried to go as much to the right, or west, as we were able. Fighting our way west was going to prove a real chore for the next two weeks.

We made better time when the winds stiffened during the night. *Courageous* was making five or six knots in a wind of twenty knots. The seas became higher, up to 6 to 8 feet, but *Courageous* rode them like a frigate as she plowed ahead into the night. We had not a clue that we were in for more than just a little blow.

Charlie and I had a mutual friend and navy pilot with whom we each had flown, Bob Davies, who was assigned as a meteorologist for the Navy in Monterey, California. Bob had tried unsuccessfully to get in touch with us prior to our departure that morning. He would have requested that we delay our departure a few days because of a strong depression developing to the southwest. There was a good possibility that it would develop into a hurricane. Hence, unbeknown to us, we were already experiencing wind on the backside of that depression, and destined for greater winds and seas.

We discovered very quickly that the person who came out from under the tarp at night to take over the watch first had to become acclimatized to sailing the raft with no visual references. The person at the helm briefed the relief person as to compass heading, and the best way that he had discovered to handle the raft in then current seas. When Charlie and I traded places, he stayed up long enough to make sure I was comfortable at the helm, and had developed a feel for what was coming from behind in the dark. Otherwise, the sound of the waves was the only clue to their direction. We would listen, then counter the force of the wave with the rudder in order to keep the raft headed downwind. The seas were reaching a very large state and we did not want to broach, i.e., to take a wave sidewise with a chance of turning over. At length I became comfortable with the feel, gained some night vision, and Charlie crawled under the tarp for his nap.

Our sleeping arrangements were confined to say the least. We had along two nylon sleeping bags, but it was so warm under the tarp we found we could take off our float coats, and lie on top of the sleeping bags or simply use the bags as pillows. Charlie actually managed to get into his sleeping bag, and zip it up saying it was down right cozy. The only thing that was to drive me bananas on the entire trip was the sound and smell of the water in our sleeping quarters. Seawater, collecting between the floorboards and the rubber bottom of the raft took on a horrible odor. It was like sleeping in the mouth of a giant toad that, having had onions and fish for dinner, burped continuously. What happened as the raft flexed with each passing wave was that a gap formed between the boards and the raft's bottom. On the backside of the wave, the raft snapped back into shape, spewing air and water vapor up through the floorboards directly into my ears and nose. In other words, the raft acted like a large bellows. It was truly disgusting, the only remedy being to sleep with my head toward the stern, darned uncomfortable to say the least. Furthermore, in this position the tarp didn't totally cover me.

Temperatures were downright cold at night. And, as the waves gained height, some of them broke against the stern to give us a good shower. With both water and air temperature at about 60 degrees, and wind blowing at 20 knots, we found it impossible to stay warm while at the helm. Therefore, it was a delightful contrast to be under the tarp, and at least halfway warm. When a wave broke into the raft the helmsmen got soaked right away, and the person under the tarp, while not getting the full blast of the shower, soon felt the water seeping first into his sleeping bag, then into his clothing.

What proved to have been a prudent choice was our purchase of wool clothing. I had found during my research why sailors wore wool clothing. Wool has the unique property of being able to retain body heat even when it is wet. We found that wool really did stay warm even when it got wet, so long as we stayed out of the wind. While I lay under the tarp, I could hear the sound of the raft plowing through the water. Bubbles flowing under the raft gave it the sound of a speedraft. We could almost estimate our speed by the sound of the water rushing under the raft. Every now and then the raft would literally fly down a wave. The sound from under the tarp resembled a barrel whooshing over a waterfall. I whooped it up as I steered the raft down the breaking waves. It was almost like surfing.

Neither of us was hungry that first day. I think we may have been just a little seasick, or the excitement of that first day out may have disguised our appetites. But of course, we had pigged out on the yacht that morning. We finally stopped talking, and Charlie went to sleep. Then I had four hours of helming *Courageous* in those seas. I was pooped when I looked at my watch, and saw that it was midnight, time for the changeover. When I roused Charlie, he complained, "Boy, did that time pass quickly!"

"Depends on your point of view," was my response as I thought my watch would never end.

Charlie wakened, still in a sleep stupor, but it was time for his watch, and he knew I was tired. He pulled himself out of the sleeping bag, and donned his coat and sock hat.

Trading places was a tricky feat. The helmsman would wedge himself into a corner of the stern to get as much of his body under the tarp as possible. Meanwhile, the emerging helmsman squeezed himself from under the tarp. The maneuver helped to keep us warm and keep the water off. When Charlie pulled the tarp aside and crawled out into the night air, he was startled to find the night so dark. There was now a heavy overcast, no stars, and no moon. I hadn't been able to see a damn thing in the surrounding sea, but gradually grew accustomed to the wind, the sound of the waves, and the motion of the raft. The lights off the coast had disappeared, and it was like the bottom of an ink well. The waves were definitely attention-getters. The wind was now a steady 25 knots, and the waves much larger than when Charlie had gone to bed. He had absolutely no feel for what the raft was doing, and couldn't understand how well I handled the raft considering that I couldn't see a thing in that abyss.

"Listen", I said, "I'll helm a little longer while you get a feel for what's happening."

"The waves are in a crossing pattern. You have to listen for their direction. Once you've figured out the direction, steer the raft down wind, and down the side of the waves."

"You've got to be shitting me, I can't see the damn waves, " Charlie yelled.

"Remember, you can't see them, you just have to feel them," I replied.

On second thought, for Charlie to take the helm without becoming comfortable with the sea conditions, he might turn the damn raft over so I decided to play it safe and stay up a little longer!

"I'll give you the helm, and I'll stay back here with you for awhile. Let me know when you feel comfortable with these waves," I said.

Thus began a routine we were to repeat often during the rest of the trip. Charlie kept waiting for his eyes to develop night vision, but there was no such thing as "night vision" out there. There were no lights from which to adapt night vision. The whole world was black. There was occasional phosphorescence in the water from the foaming waves, but it didn't help. Just more of the proverbial ink well, except this ink well was moving and dangerous.

We managed to change positions with the raft becoming a bucking bronco. I held the rudder steady until Charlie got seated in the raft. He still had not developed a feel for what was happening. A couple of times the waves caught the raft by the stern quarter, and gave it a good push sideways before he countered with the rudder. In about ten minutes, he started to get the feel, but still worried that he couldn't see the waves coming. Finally, he began to listen for them, and prepared to rudder in the proper direction. I could see that Charlie liked to take them at an angle, while I had found it easier to helm the raft with the stern directly to the face of the waves.

Charlie soon realized that this overlapping of the watch cut into my rest time so he told me that he, "had it now," and that I could turn in. It was colder than a well digger's ass, and I was happy to crawl under the tarp and out of the wind. Neither of us had brought gloves, so we became adept at handling the rudder with one hand while warming the other in a pocket. Helming the raft in the large waves was work, furiously hard work. As the raft surfed down the waves, their force against the rudder took a tremendous amount of effort to counteract. The rudder had to be held deep in the water to keep the raft going down wind, and down the side of the waves. The raft accelerated up to ten knots on each wave, creating a powerful force against the rudder. It was the main reason I chose to go stern to the waves. Less effort was needed to keep the raft going directly down the side of the wave than by running at an angle, and maybe a treacherous angle at that.

By three o'clock the morning of July 5th, the wind increased to 30 knots. We had no way to estimate the waves accurately, but they were getting big. Charlie yelled that they were towering over the raft, and were beginning to sound like locomotives as they crashed by. Every now and then a "crasher" would break against the raft, and douse *Courageous* with gallons of cold water. We weren't in any danger of sinking, but the water was so cold! It soaked everything, including Charlie and me. There was absolutely nothing we could do to avoid the breaking waves. We simply sat there in turbulent blackness, listened for them, and hoped that they would give us a good push instead of breaking against us.

Charlie worked his ass off trying to helm *Courageous*. "Shit," I thought to myself, "with this kind of speed we'll reach Hawaii in a month." We must have been making a steady eight to ten knots, sometimes a whole lot faster as we surfed down some of the larger waves. I lay there thirsty as hell, but there was no water. The sky cleared some, and every now and then Charlie said he could see a star. I began to get sleepy so I told Charlie to get me up if he needed help. Otherwise I was going to try to get some sleep.

"George, its time to get up."

That's how long it seemed I slept. Time raced by for the guy trying to rest, and crawled for the guy at the helm.

Boy, I was tired! But I had to get up and get dressed. Charlie had been fighting the wind and waves for four hours. He looked frozen. His hands and fingers were numb. He had to have been as dehydrated as I.

What a shock I was in for when I pulled the tarp off! Now the waves were even larger than when I went to bed, and the wind a steady thirty-five knots. The raft screamed along like a banshee out of control. We had to be averaging over ten knots. I gave a rough estimate that we were about ten to fifteen miles north of Monterey, and somewhere in the neighborhood of sixty miles west of the nearest land. Nothing was visible except an occasional star. The water was totally black except for the occasional phosphorescence in the waves.

"I'm dead tired. Its all yours," Charlie said as he began to move over and give me the helm. Had he forgotten that I had absolutely no idea or feel for what was going on around me? The only comparison I could make was the disorientation of first going "under the hood" in Navy instrument flight training. A bag or "hood" pulled over the cockpit obliterates all outside references. The pilot must then refer to the instrument panel to determine the plane's attitude. But in this blackness, except for the occasional glimpse of a star, there was no way of telling which side was up or down. There were no visual cues for maintaining equilibrium. No instrument panel.

"I can't see shit!" I yelled.

"No problem, just keep her headed downwind."

"Wait, you helm until I can get a feel for what's going on."

Charlie broke out into a big laugh. He knew exactly what I was experiencing, and he decided to have a devilish good joke on me.

"You asshole," I laughed.

Charlie continued to helm the raft for about ten more minutes, while I sat there thinking he was probably the greatest sailor in the world for being able to handle the raft so masterfully in these waves and wind, yet not able to see a thing beyond arm's length.

Continually amazing to me, was the speed at which each of us adapted to helming the rudder in the building seas and wind. Charlie had no problem by now in anticipating the waves just from the feel of the raft, and the sound of the waves coming up behind us. When I finally took the helm, I struggled for a while to regain the feel I had prior to my nap. It was down right scary. Monster waves came roaring by. They had built to between twenty to twenty-five feet! Some of them broke into the raft, and not just against the side. The raft was swamped in water. It was useless to bail. Another wave would come along and dump in more gallons.

Charlie crawled under the tarp, and got into his sleeping bag. He remarked how much easier the ride as he lay there in the bottom of the raft as compared to helming in the wind and water, a pretty rough comparison considering that he lay there with all his gear and clothing soaked.

I was overwhelmed by the size of the waves that came crashing by. Their sound, rather, roar was terrific. The sound was likened to a locomotive careening down the tracks toward us. It was spooky to know they were coming, and have no way to make them out until they were looming behind, then feel nothing but foaming white water. I sat there looking aft trying to pierce the dark to get the best idea possible of the direction the next big one was coming from. The wind direction stayed constant, but the waves were turbulent, sometimes coming from the right, and then from the left. At first I thought my headings were varying with the waves, but I checked the compass again and again, and saw that we were maintaining a fairly constant heading.

What we were experiencing is known as, "crossing seas." One wave comes from the left and another from the right. Usually the result of proximity to a land mass, wave motion literally bouncing off a land mass, changing direction as it flows outward. The outgoing wave then crosses over the next incoming wave, and so on, causing the sailors' "crossing seas."

I waited until I saw the next wave approach very close by, then made an instant adjustment with the rudder to turn the stern into the wave. All hell broke loose. As the wave approached, the sail popped with the force of the wind, and the aft end of the raft bucked up. With the bow pointing down and the stern up, we accelerated with the wave. I held rudder with all my strength to keep the raft headed down the side of the wave. If we broached in these conditions, we would surely be overturned!

Once the wave passed, the sail flapped again as it lost wind in the wave's trough, then the cycle started all over again. I realized that we were in much more wind than was normal for that time of year, but I also realized that if we had these kinds of winds, we would never have the energy left to helm the raft after a few weeks. It took every bit of energy we could muster to helm for four hours in such conditions.

I was too inexperienced, or too excited about the speed we were making to evaluate the real, potential danger we were in. It crossed my mind that we ought to put out the five sea anchors we carried, and drop sail, at least until morning when we could see what was coming at us. We simply lacked the experience to make the kind of judgment needed for this situation. Besides, it was only the first day at sea and I didn't want to stop sailing the first day. We had too far to go. In one way, it seemed stupid to stop our apparent progress. Pilot charts indicate that average winds in these oceans are eleven to sixteen knots. But we were now in constant thirty-five to forty knot winds. The raft seemed to be handling well, even though it was pretty wild coming down the face of some of those waves. If we stopped now, it might take much longer to reach Hawaii than we had planned. I also thought there was a good chance of our encountering days with no wind, so better to take advantage of the big wind we had in order to average out the no-wind days.

By dawn on July 5, my 29th birthday, I estimated that we were abeam Monterey, and perhaps no more than eighty miles from land. The waves were awesome. They towered above *Courageous*. It was hard to imagine, when looking up at them, that the raft could rise fast enough to keep from being buried beneath an avalanche of water. *Courageous* was making great time! "Guestimating" the speed by the wake we made, we were averaging at least ten knots. We careened down the side of the waves doing fifteen to twenty knots, then slowed to almost a stop as we were left in the trough between waves. It was one hell of a ride.

These were probably the highest winds we encountered on the entire trip. Whenever the wind got above thirty knots, Charlie and I considered it a "storm" no matter if the sky were crystal blue or cloudy. The reason for our "storm" description had more to do with wave action danger whenever the wind got above thirty knots. And believe me, on the Pacific in a raft, it is a storm when the winds reach thirty knots or more. The wind and waves had become dangerous. We didn't, however perversely, consider ourselves in any danger at this point, ignorance being bliss. In our Navy flying we had been taught and trained to know the limits of our aircraft, and to operate within those limits. However, in aerial combat practice the only way to know the limit was to push beyond the limit, which meant we often temporarily lost control of the aircraft. I vividly remember on one of my air-to-air combat training flights I was flying against a Commander who had lots of actual combat experience. I remember the effort it took to get on his "six". I was totally fearless when flying, and the A-4 Skyhawk I flew in the training command was a super plane to fly. The cockpit was so small that we kidded that you didn't get in the plane, you put it on. I was just about to get into "firing" position behind the Commander's aircraft when all of a sudden he just dropped out of the sky. I shot past him and figured he had some trick up his sleeve that I hadn't learned yet. Wow! What a move he put on me. Back at the base for our debrief, I asked what maneuver he had performed when I was about to get into firing position. He said, "maneuver my ass, hell I scared the shit out of myself, entered an accelerated stall, and damn near punched out before I got control of the plane." So that was what happened, he had stalled. There is no way in the world to follow a plane that stalled. I put that into my memory bank, that if I was ever in a situation where the enemy had gained position on me, a stall might be one way to at least get out of trouble to fight again another day. The point of the story, however, is to explain that in aviation we learned that aircraft have what we call a "flight envelope" in which the aircraft can be operated safely. That day in the training command the Commander pushed the envelope and departed flight. Our lack of experience as sailors would now lead us into a situation that was about to culminate in near disaster, as we were about to push the "sailing envelope" pass the limits.

There was once a well-respected scholar and philosopher who was eulogized for his good judgment. When asked how he happened to come about such impeccably good judgment he answered "experience from poor judgment". Well, we were about to get a heavy dose of poor judgment that led us to a lot better judgment later in the trip.

Charlie woke up early, and we were both enjoying the ride. I'd been at the helm for almost four hours, bone tired but excited. At eight o'clock Charlie and I traded places. Tired but not sleepy, I stayed up awhile to watch the show. Everything in the raft was soaking wet. I tried to bail out some of the water so I could rest better when I got under the tarp. If we both sat on the same side of the raft, the water would run to that side, and I could bail with one of the plastic jars packed in the survival kit.

I saw things that day that I wouldn't have believed had I not been there. We discovered that once the wind got up to thirty knots or better, and blew steadily, it took about four hours of that wind before large waves formed. The wind had been blowing for almost eight hours now, and the waves were something to behold: towering over twenty feet, and some even much larger. I've heard of rough waves, but those waves were taller than just "rough," they were fury let loose! The wave and wind noise was unbelievable. At dawn, we finally could see the waves building to our rear. They swelled up like monsters, ready to engulf us.

The raft rose up on the side of the waves, and swooped down the side, accelerating all the while. Suddenly we looked back to see one particularly large, building wave. We didn't like the looks of it because it was "out of sync" with the normal wave motion. It kept building and building. This thing was different! It didn't seem to want to stop building until it became a vertical wall of water behind us. I mean, and this is no shit, the wave was 35 feet above us, and it was going to come cascading down right on top of us. There was no way *Courageous* could rise to this wave. There was nothing to rise to. There was no front part to it. It was literally a vertical wall of water. The wave finally broke, and more water came down on us than imaginable. There was nothing we could do but hang on. In river rafting we called raging rapids "white water". This was "white water" all right, and it was all over us.

There wasn't anything Charlie could do to handle the raft. He kept the rudder as deep as possible, but *Courageous* plunged somewhat side ways in the rush of the "white water" as it passed over us. The whole world was out of control! That wave meant to be Mother Nature's way of telling us that we were about to get the shit kicked out of us. Instead of pulling down the sail, and putting the sea anchors out, we kept sailing. We were dumbly driven to make it to Hawaii, and we were not about to stop sailing when we had what might be the best wind of the trip. Oh no! In the Navy when a pilot had an accident on his way home to friends and family because he had pushed himself beyond safe limits, we called it, "get-home-itis". I guess what we had was, "get-to-Hawaii-itis".

I bailed water, and finally crawled under the tarp at about nine o'clock. I took my float jacket off, and slid into my sleeping bag. It was wet, but soon warmed with the heat of my body. The gurgling noise and the smell were the pits, but there was nothing I could do about that. The sound of the water rushing beneath the raft as she came down the waves was beauty to my ears, and I suspected that we would be ahead of schedule in getting to Hawaii. Every now and then Charlie would yell, "Standby for whitewater!", meaning that we were about to get a dousing from the next wave to break into, or directly onto the stern of the raft. I could hear and feel the water as it splashed against the tarp, pushing it against me. It wasn't more than a second after I heard the water that I felt it penetrate my sleeping bag, then a few minutes later, the bag would become warm again.

I really couldn't sleep. The noise was terrible, if not terrifying, and the frequent, cold sea water hammering the raft was more than a chilly awakening. I rested, and if no water hit the raft for a few minutes, I may have dozed off a few times. The clouds had burned off, and it was a beautiful, clear day. We'd put the solar stills to work. I surely looked forward to that first drink of water. The two of us were very thirsty. We still had had nothing to eat, and were getting a little hungry. During the night we each had a bowel movement, and we had urinated over the side. Confounding the urge to eliminate was our effort to find a safe position on that wild ride. We ended up hanging our butts over the stern by the rudder, an acrobatic balancing act, and not very comfortable to say the least.

At about ten o'clock, Charlie yelled, "Standby for whitewater!" as he caught sight of a large wave building to the stern. I was pissed to get soaked again, but there wasn't anything I could do. I felt the raft's stern begin to rise with the wave. Charlie's legs stiffened against me, and I felt him bracing himself trying to keep the rudder in the water. The raft was rising rapidly, much more than normal. I could see nothing, but could hear the noise of the wave as the raft began to accelerate. The "G" force pushed me to the floor. Something was not right! Water began to pound against the tarp, and I knew we were going stern over bow. An upset! I was bounced around inside the raft like a ping pong ball. The motion stopped, and the noise stopped. The raft was still. I was on top of the tarp, and the bottom of the raft was over me. The darkness under the raft disoriented me. I knew one thing: I couldn't move, and I was definitely in the water.

My thin nylon sleeping bag was zipped up around my shoulders, and clung to me like a wet tee shirt. I was frantic to get out of the sleeping bag so I could swim. Without my float coat on, I was sinking further into the water. After a few seconds, which felt like minutes, I was able to get my shoulders out of the bag and my arms free, but I was all tangled up in the lines and still had the damn bag around my feet. I pulled at the tarp so that I could get out of the raft. I shall never forget what my eyes saw when I got the tarp off. I was staring into clear blue water, as far down as I could see. I saw the underwater camera case float away, turning lazy loops as it drifted down into the deep blue water. I saw my float coat that I'd been using as a pillow, and I grabbed it. I kicked the sleeping bag free, and swam under the pontoons to get away from the lines and the raft. Once I was well away from the raft, I swam to the side and surfaced. Quickly slipping into my float coat, I got my bearings.

Everything had become so quiet for those few seconds while under the raft, I forgot the storm raging above. I was about to be reminded that Mother Nature and the sea are relentless foes. It's not like a prize fight, when you're knocked down and out, the fight's over. No, in this sea, the sea kicks your butt, you go down, and it keeps on kicking. I surfaced only to be greeted by the noise, and the raging water. *Courageous* was bottom up. The sight was frightening. I couldn't see Charlie anywhere.

"Charlie! Charlie! Charlieeeeeeeeee!" I yelled. It was hopeless. I could barely hear my own voice over the noise of wind and waves. The wind felt as if it were shoving the words right back down my throat. There was no sound but wind and waves. I swam toward *Courageous* and made my way to the stern. At the stern, I could see around the side of the raft, and there was Charlie swimming toward *Courageous*.

"Are you OK?" I shouted. He gave me a thumbs up, and he asked how I was. I gave him a thumbs up. We were in serious trouble, however, and we both knew it. We knew our survival time was not more than two or three hours in the cold water. The bottom of *Courageous* was covered with small barnacles from being in San Francisco Bay for so many weeks prior to our trip. We pulled ourselves over the stern, and onto the bottom. It was warmer, but we had to devise a plan of action quickly.

We each cut our hands and legs on the barnacles, not badly, but they were bleeding. We grabbed what we could from the water, but saw that we had lost some equipment, and we didn't know if *Courageous* had sustained damage. I was sure that *Courageous* would have some very serious, unrepairable damage. That's how violently we had been thrown over. We did see one piece of critical equipment float away, the solar still. I was tempted to swim after it, but it bounced across the water so fast in the wind that I would never have caught up to it. The fresh water in the still, so important to us, was blowing away. I had just swallowed a lot of sea water, and it wasn't sitting too well in my stomach.

"How far out do you think we are?" Charlie asked.

"I think we're just south of Monterey, maybe a hundred miles out to sea. We might be close to a shipping lane, but we can't stay out here like this for long," I answered.

The sun was still bright, and we had the balance of the day to figure out what we were going to do. We certainly had to get a move on because the wind chill factor was beginning to numb our hands and fingers.

I had to mention the obvious. " We could call the Coast Guard on the emergency radios, and let them know we're in trouble." I absolutely hated that idea because I knew I would have to face the Commander, and listen to his, "I told you so" speech. Here we were, only the second day out, and had a major problem. I felt responsible for Charlie, even though he had volunteered to come with me. After all, I had planned the trip, and designed the survival kit. I thought Charlie deserved a say in whether or not to call the Coast Guard if he wanted to quit.

"Hell no!" Charlie replied. "I wouldn't give the bastards the satisfaction, besides that, we don't even know if we still have the radios."

"OK." I agreed, "Let's get the raft upright, and take stock of what we still have. I think the life rafts are still under the spray hood. If they are, we can get in them, and flip *Courageous* over. If we both get on the same side, we can lift one side up, and flip her over."

We had to get back into the water in order to reach under *Courageous* and release the two, one-person rafts. We had two one-person life rafts for emergencies, and this was an emergency. We pulled the inflation cords, and the CO_2 bottles quickly inflated the rafts. Once inside the tiny rafts, and with both of us on the same side of *Courageous*, we lifted with all our strength. But we weren't budging it. Instead of lifting *Courageous*, we were forcing the smaller rafts under water. I couldn't believe the weight of *Courageous*. But it wasn't really the weight, it was the suction being created under the raft every time we tried to lift it. We couldn't seem to break the suction. We tried for about 45 minutes to turn *Courageous* upright. I was sick, and so was Charlie, from the shear physical effort. We had put every bit of energy we had into trying to lift *Courageous*. It's unbelievable the amount of strength available if your life is hanging in the balance. In the midst of this, I threw up, and began to feel a little better. We were both so worn out. We each took time-out to rest in our one-person rafts while holding on to *Courageous*. We tied the rafts together, secured them to *Courageous*, and climbed back onto *Courageous'* bottom. We had to recapture some strength before we could go on tugging and lifting.

The wind blew, and the waves broke over us. With the little rest I'd had during the night and on top of getting sick, I started to get pissed. I wasn't going to quit, and I didn't intend to die sitting on an overturned raft!

"Listen," I said to Charlie, "Let's deflate one of the side chambers, and turn the raft around so the other chamber is upwind. If we can then lift the raft just enough to break the suction, maybe the wind will catch it, and help flip her over."

I swam under *Courageous* and released some of the air in the main inflation chamber. We got back into the one-person rafts, and swam the raft around so she was broadside to the wind and waves. Once more we tried, with every last ounce of strength, to lift the raft. We broke the suction, but could only lift her about a foot. That was it! The harder we tried, the deeper our rafts went into the water. Waves pounded us relentlessly. We climbed back on top of *Courageous*.

We were both sick, and hypothermia was setting in. My fingers were so numb that I couldn't zip my float coat. I was positive that we could get *Courageous* upright, but how? We were desperate now, and didn't have time to mess around. We'd been in the water for over two hours, and the situation was becoming dangerous.

As we sat discussing whether or not to get back into the rafts, to try and lift again, something in the water caught my eye. I sat bolt upright, and yelled for Charlie to look. There was a fin breaking the surface of the water very near us. We looked around, and saw fins everywhere.

"Shark all around us," I yelled. "Look at them." I hadn't actually seen a shark, only the fins breaking the water.

"Sunfish! They're sunfish," Charlie said. "Look over there!" He pointed to a huge fish lying more or less on its side, and very near the surface. The fins we were seeing were pectoral fins which break the surface when the sun fish lie on their sides.

These were huge sunfish. They looked to be about three to four feet wide, and about the same length. My first thought was, food.

"Look how close they're coming," I said. "I bet we could catch one, or shoot it with the spear. Are sunfish good to eat?"

"I never heard of anyone eating sunfish, it's supposed to be real bony, and not much meat," Charlie replied.

"A fish that big has got to have some meat on it. Let's get this raft upright. Maybe we can catch one", I replied.

For the moment the fish had drawn our attention from the fact that we were still in big trouble. Food wouldn't matter if we didn't get *Courageous* upright. I finally made the decision that I knew I had to make. We were desperate, and desperate action was going to be required, or we would have to call for help.

"Charlie" I said, "if we totally deflate *Courageous* I think we can pull her over herself then put her back together."

"You mean deflate the floatation chambers?" Charlie quizzed.

"Yes. I don't think there's any way that we'd let so much air out to let her sink. Once she's deflated, we'll reach over and put our feet or knees on one chamber, and pull the next chamber toward us. That way we won't have to lift the raft off the water."

"Lets give it a try", Charlie agreed.

"I'll go under the raft, and find the foot pump. If we've lost the pump we might have to re-think our plan. It'll be nearly impossible to refill the chambers without the pump. When I find the pump I'll hand it up to you, then I'll pull the plugs and begin deflating the chambers. As the chambers deflate, I'll hand you the floor-boards and any loose gear."

Charlie agreed. He pulled the one-person rafts close by, and tied them to *Courageous* so he could use them to hold the equipment that I handed to him. I really wasn't looking forward to getting back in the water, but I didn't have a choice. I had planned this trip, and I had to take the responsibility and the chances. Because I was cut and bleeding, I told Charlie to watch for shark, if he should see any, to beat on the bottom of the raft. I wasn't too concerned with a sneak attack, because I figured I could see at least eighty to a hundred feet through the water. But I was going to be busy, and I didn't want to have to worry about looking for something I really didn't want to see.

I slipped into the water and dove under *Courageous*. I swam to the bow where I knew the foot pump should have been. My heart was really pounding especially when I didn't find the pump right away. I was praying that the pump had not broken loose and sunk. But finally I saw the pump in a dark corner of the bow. I let out a yell, and Charlie knew I had found the pump. I could breath under the raft as there was about six inches of air space between the water and the bottom of the raft. I dove back under, and came up to hand Charlie the pump. We were both all smiles. Now we had a chance.

Back under *Courageous*, I gathered any articles floating around, and handed them to Charlie who was having his own problems. While he tried to keep all the gear together, the wind blew things away, or the waves knocked them out of the one-person rafts. He tied off what he could, and stuffed the rest in the bottom of one of the rafts.

When I located the first inflation chamber, I twisted the valve off, and air rushed out with a loud "whoosh." I moved to the other valves, twisting them off one by one. Slowly the bottom of the raft began to collapse on my head. When all the chambers were deflated, I replaced the valves, and swam to the surface. We didn't waste a lot of time getting into action when I got to the surface. Charlie had finished tying off all the gear. Both of us got on top of *Courageous*, and using our bodies as levers, reached across to grab the line on the farthest inflation tube. Pushing with our legs, we pulled the raft over itself. *Courageous* looked odd just flopping limp in the water, just barely above the surface. A vision did cross my mind of *Courageous* getting away from us and filling with just enough water to start to sink. If that happened, there was no way we would ever get her to the surface again. Charlie and I threw ourselves into the work of pulling *Courageous* upright. We did it. Finally, *Courageous* was upright. She was floating about two inches above the water, but she was floating and she was upright.

With the raft now upright, we replaced the floor-boards. Installing those floor-boards had been difficult on land, but here in twenty-five foot waves it was a mortal challenge. The work was so intense that I'd even forgot about being cold. We both worked double time, and things started coming together. Once the floor-boards were in place, we attached the inflation hose from the foot pump to the first valve. Since we couldn't stand up to pump with our feet, we had to hold the foot pump and pump with our hands. It took a long time, but we finally managed to re-inflate *Courageous* and set up housekeeping.

We began to survey *Courageous* for damage. The plank that held the lee-boards had cracked, but we could live with that. There were no rips in the raft, and the inflation chambers were not leaking. Now we had to re-rig *Courageous*.

First, we broke out our two remaining solar stills, mounting one on either of the two aft inflation chambers. We were so dehydrated from the episode in the water, plus the lack of drinking water during the first day that we needed water badly. We still had a complete survival kit, since the kit was tied to the raft. With the re-packing finished, it was about two in the afternoon, and the sun was bright in clear skies. With any luck we would have some water by sundown. We found the sea anchors, and tied them to the corners of the raft. Even without the sail, *Courageous* still wanted to surf down the side of the big waves. We had one large sea anchor which we attached to the bow lifting handle. *Courageous* would now ride with bow into the wind and waves, and we no longer accelerated down the side of the waves.

The sunfish were still in the area, so we thought some fishing was in order. If sunfish were not the best eating fish it didn't matter, because they might be our best and only chance for food, and I didn't relish wasting that chance. We had no bait to attract the fish, so we took out the, "Hawaiian Sling" to try and shoot a fish. They looked like awfully dumb fish, but they knew we were after them. The spear was effective for about ten feet, and the fish stayed just out of range. We shot at them a few times, but they swam even further away. We stalked them for thirty minutes or so, and finally gave up.

We finished putting things away, and secured the raft, again carefully inspecting *Courageous* for damage. The mast hadn't broken, but the lug pole that held the sail had busted. I had to laugh about the lug pole. Just before I stepped off our houseboat to take the raft to Jack London Square the day before, I noticed a mop sitting on the porch. I took the mop handle, and told Judi that it might come in handy as a spare. For the balance of 54 days we used that mop handle as a lug pole to hold the sail in place. I was surely glad I grabbed Judi's mop!

There were no tears or holes in *Courageous* and she seemed to be holding air okay. We may have lost a lot of equipment, but we still had the survival kit, and that was what we were out here for in the first place. On inventory, we lost one sleeping bag, some clothing, and Charlie's sock-hat was gone. The underwater cameras were gone, one solar still had blown away, and some of the medical and emergency equipment was missing. The sail had a slight tear in one corner, but nothing that we couldn't overcome. We had taken one hell of a knockdown. The raft had come through it okay, and the survival kit was intact.

Once Charlie and I were convinced the raft was OK and that she rode the waves safely, we realized how absolutely tired and cold we were. We reattached the tarp, and both of us crawled under it, and into the one remaining sleeping bag, curling up against each other in a fetal position. This was no time for modesty or inhibitions. We both were dangerously chilled. I couldn't stop my teeth from chattering. Everything was soaked to the last thread, but slowly we began to warm.

Charlie and I never talked about quitting. We reflected on two facts: first, that we hadn't lost the survival kit, and second, that we had just gained an experience that we each knew was lacking to the expedition; i.e. trauma. No one could now say that our trip lacked the kind of trauma that puts a castaway into a life raft. Our lives had just hung in balance. If anything, the expedition was now more realistic than ever. We were more than a trifle discouraged, as much about our seamanship as anything else. We were about as deflated as our raft had been. We had even lost that resolute commitment to make it all the way to Hawaii. So we decided to just stick with it a few more days, and see how things went. We talked about getting the radios out to let the Coast Guard know what had happened, then thought better of it. We agreed that it would be better not to tell anyone until after the trip was over.

Even though we were under the tarp, we could hear the waves approaching. The raft would lift, start to accelerate, the sea anchor would catch, and then the movement would stop. It was not a comfortable ride, but it felt safe. At about dark, we climbed out from under the tarp to check the solar stills. We had some fresh water, but precious little. We each had a little less than four ounces to quench a huge thirst. With darkness coming on, we checked over everything to make sure we were not going to be in for any surprises.

When the night settled in, we crawled back under the tarp, and into the sleeping bag. The wind had let up to about thirty knots, but the waves still rolled as high as before. Every few minutes a huge splash of water landed on the tarp, then we would feel the new, soaking cold as water flowed into the raft and over us. We tried to pull the tarp tight so that the water would flow over the sides of the raft, but there was so much water that some of it would always find its way into the raft.

The worst of two people having to sleep in the same sleeping bag is the turning. When one person wants to move, both have to move. No sooner would one of us go to sleep than the other said he had to turn. I would sleep on my side until it hurt so badly it felt like someone was driving nails into my hip and shoulder. I hated to wake Charlie to turn, but once it became too torturous to bear, I would wake him, and we would turn over. Charlie felt the same way when he had to wake me, but we understood and accepted it as something we were going to live with for awhile.

All night the wind and waves bounced us around. A couple of times during the night we had to bail out some water, because it got into our ears, noses, and mouths, generally making our night even more miserable. Any move at all became a tremendous effort. We had first, to extract ourselves from the wet sleeping bag, then move around in the dark. We didn't even try to urinate over the side anymore. We took one of the survival kit jars, urinated in it, and threw the urine over the side. That took a whole lot less effort than trying to hang over the side in the wind and waves.

I mentioned previously of reading that castaways or various sects drank urine, and that it is not helpful to do so in a survival situation. The human kidney works at a very high efficiency level, and waste material in urine is filtered to such a high degree that to drink it adds nothing to the hydration of the body. Neither of us even gave a thought to drinking our urine, and I would say, we were extremely thirsty.

This night seemed to last forever. We slept because we were so damnably exhausted. Every time we heard a large wave coming, we tensed. The prospect of the raft turning over again made it difficult to relax. I kept hoping the wind would die down so we could have some peace and quiet.

At first light I crawled out of the sleeping bag, and out from under the tarp. The sea anchor on the bow had taken a tremendous beating all night, and I wanted to check for chafing. Everything seemed to be in order. The wind was still up to twenty-five knots, and the swells were twenty feet with larger ones from time to time. Charlie got up shortly afterwards, and we discussed the merits of putting up the sail. We both agreed that in consideration of the high waves, sailing would be foolish. Pushed along by wind and current, we were nevertheless making progress to the south. There wasn't much to do except to keep the solar stills inflated and full of sea water.

Still near exhaustion, we just wanted to rest. It was a clear day, and all I could think about was getting a drink from the solar still. Waves continued to pound us hour after hour. Once in a while we bailed the cold water out of the raft to keep warm. Charlie's wool sock-hat, lost when we overturned, left him bare-headed and exposed to losing more body heat than I. Physiologists say that one can lose up to thirty percent of body heat through the head. Charlie eventually retrieved his white sailor's hat from below, and it helped, but not so much as the wool sock-hat.

At noon we decided to have our first meal. Mealtime became a ritual for the rest of the trip until we ran out of food. We would open the food container, and take out one piece of candy each. Not much of a meal, but it tasted good, and created some saliva in our mouths. We "ate" slowly, as if this were a real banquet. We talked about the waves, and how long we thought these conditions might last. Our first disagreement centered on how best to take the waves. I was convinced that we had overturned because of Charlie's habit of taking the seas on our aft quarter, sliding down the waves sideways. I thought it better to keep the raft square to the waves with the stern dead on to the coming waves. Each view had its good points, but in reality it wouldn't have made any difference. Some of the rougher waves were over forty feet tall! The sheer vertical drop on the front side of such waves would cause havoc no matter where the stern pointed.

Very carefully we extracted water from the solar stills. They had made almost ten ounces of water, and we divided it evenly. It was our first full drink since turning over; great, but not nearly enough. Some salt water had contaminated the water, but with the motion of the raft, it proved impossible to keep salt water out completely. We refilled the stills with saltwater, thirstily anticipating an evening drink.

On this third afternoon, we reached a conclusion that our

trip was going to be hard enough without disagreement, and that in order to survive we would have to cooperate and pull together. We never quibbled or disagreed after that. We made a pact to save all differences until after the trip, and that's what we did. I was surely glad I hadn't packed games in the survival kit, because I could see how they might be the potential cause of some really disagreeable feelings in a life raft situation.

Late that afternoon it seemed that the wind had decreased a little, so we decided to put up the sail and see how the raft handled. We pulled the large sea anchor in, as well as the four sea anchors under the raft. Charlie took the helm and I moved forward to pull the sail up on its new mop lug pole. The raft started moving very quickly. In not too long a time however, the first large wave came thundering down upon us, and again we accelerated more or less under control down its side. Zooming down the side of the waves no longer held its "fun" appeal as before. We understood all too well what could happen.

When the action stopped, Charlie and I looked at each other with one conscious opinion, let's stop this sailing and put out the sea anchors again. Turning over that second day out was probably the best thing that could have happened to Charlie and me. Being only the second day, we had had enough strength to fight and put the raft upright. If it had happened four weeks later, I'm not sure we would have had enough strength left to swat a fly. We learned a valuable lesson, and wouldn't take any more chances like that again. We encountered four other storms at sea during the next two months, but fortunately, never turned the raft over, even though we came close to it a couple of times.

Once more we dropped the sail, and put out the sea anchors. But now I had a new worry. The cuts on my feet were swelling. They didn't necessarily look infected or filled with puss, but they were so swollen they looked like leather in water. There seemed to be layers of new skin trying to form, but they weren't scabbing over. They just stayed wet, and boy, were they sensitive!

My feet became so painful if I rubbed them against anything that I finally had to remove my underwear to wrap around them. It helped a good deal, and made it at least possible for me to rest at night. I could well appreciate the descriptions given by castaways of their agony in enduring salt-water sores. The entire body weakens from fighting infections, and further weakens when rest and sleep cannot be had. Looking at the brighter side, the clothing we wore over our legs and torso prevented any further problems with salt-water sores. The importance of clothing cannot be over-emphasized, not only for thermal value but for the protection of skin.

We weren't seeing much reason for keeping our four-hour watch schedule, since we were far west of shipping lanes. Keeping a watch was just too tiring when there was nothing to do. Nights seemed to last forever. If only the waves and wind would have let up, but they continued to make life miserable for us. The morning of July 7th, the wind and waves still had us under sea anchor. I was becoming concerned that we would have these winds and waves for the entire trip. It was hard not to lose patience with the weather. I cussed the pilot charts that showed a "Force 4" wind for this place and date. "Force 4" on a meteorological wind scale means that we should have been experiencing a wind between eleven and sixteen knots that induce small waves with fairly frequent white caps. We had twice that much wind! I cussed the fact that we weren't making any real progress to the west because the damnable wind kept blowing us almost due south.

I woke up at the break of dawn, and saw a beautiful sunrise. As I busily inspected the sea anchors, something in the water caught my eye. Looking closer, I definitely saw something in the water and it electrified me. It was a small tiger shark, and it was circling *Courageous*! I yelled at Charlie and told him we had a shark circling us. It didn't take Charlie long to appear, and together we watched the shark circle not more than a foot under the raft.

I knew it was possible to catch and eat shark. Thor Heyerdahl wrote in *Kon Tiki* that one method for catching shark seemed to work very well. Heyerdahl found that if a shark were caught by the tail, and kept immobile for a few minutes, they became somewhat docile, and could be pulled aboard. Shark do not have air bladders as most fish do, and must continue to swim or sink. Notwithstanding the fact that some shark can bask motionless on the bottom, most shark do not have muscular gills, and they must continue to move through the water in order to circulate water through their gills to extract oxygen. When Heyerdahl held the shark, they became docile because they suffered from a lack of oxygen. I wanted this shark. Not only did I want the food, but I also wanted to demonstrate that shark could be caught and brought aboard an inflatable. I was at the stern, and the shark swam under the stern tubes, then circled towards the bow. I told Charlie to get an oar ready to shove in the shark's mouth in case we couldn't handle it. Charlie was not as eager as I to get this shark. I understood his reticence. The shark could cause a great deal of problems for us if it got out of hand. We would have to hold the shark firmly, and kill it as quickly as possible. I intended to grab the shark's tail as it slid by on its trip to the bow. I couldn't see the whole shark from the stern, but only part of him as he swam by. His head would appear, and his body slid by in a glance. I asked Charlie to tell me when the shark was coming back my way, because by the time I saw its head, it was too late to grab the tail. After trying a couple of tries, I only succeeded in touching the animal and scaring him away.

I was totally hyper, I wanted that shark. Charlie told me he was glad the shark got away, because he thought it was a lot bigger than I had realized. He noticed that when it swam under the bow, he could see its head on one side and its tail on the other. Considering that *Courageous* is six feet wide, the shark would have been over six feet long! Tiger shark are not broad, but rather slender, and I had not guessed that he was that long. It may be to our good fortune that I didn't grab and try to hold that one.

We spent the good part of the morning talking about our shark experience, and wondered if there were more sharks circling us at night. I became a lot more aware of what was in the water around us after that. The wind and waves were still high, but we had to get moving. We talked it over, and decided we could probably sail during the day since we could see what was coming at us. We could always lower the sail or let it go if the raft got out of control. We placed the sea anchor in a position where the person at the helm could throw it over quickly if necessary. Once again we raised the sail and got under way.

We re-established our four hour watch schedule, not because we wanted to keep watch, but because four hours was about as much as the helmsman could take. Ruddering the raft for four hours was very demanding work, and cried out for relief. At last we were moving again. There were still the exciting moments when the raft accelerated, and one of its sides began to rise out of the water. We were "spring loaded" for that eventuality however, and would immediately jump to the side of the raft that lifted up.

As we gained more experience sailing, we began to realize that it was easier to control the heading of the raft by moving the sail from side to side than it was to turn the rudder. Furthermore, we grew more and more confident in our sailing and feel of the raft as we sailed. But when it got dark, we pulled the sail down and put the sea anchors out. It wasn't worth the worry to try and sail in the high waves at night. Almost two weeks of this routine went by. I cursed the pilot charts every time I got them out. Where were those "Force 4" winds?

After that first week, we fell into a steady routine, four hours on the helm, four hours off, but only during the day. Neither of us rested well at night because of the continuous water splashing into the raft. Then too, we were probably getting more rest than if we had been standing four hour watches at night. For days we would wake up, hoist the sail, and sail during the day, taking down the sail at night, and put out sea anchors.

We had absolutely no exercise routine planned for the trip. Positive that we would lose a great deal of weight on the trip, we had intended to keep activity down. Intended, that is. Since we were to be getting only 100 calories each per day, there was little doubt that we would use our body mass as food.

The only exercise we had was that required to maintain life. We had to rudder the raft, which was to change shortly, and we had to keep the solar stills inflated and full of sea water. Other than these chores, we used a lot of energy in changing positions. We each remained in resting condition as much as possible. In the beginning, we talked a lot during the days, but talking takes energy, with a corresponding loss of water vapor. Our mouths became even drier when we talked, so we gave up talking for the most part during the day.

My pictures show that we lost great amounts of body weight, however, our shoulders, arms, and chest regions didn't suffer the muscle loss that our legs did. That was because we were still using muscles in our arms and chest. Only once did we stand up or use our legs on the trip. After two weeks with little food, we were definitely much weaker. It was an effort to move around. In fact we often elected to sit in an uncomfortable position for hours rather than burn the energy to move about.

The one effort that was absolutely wearing us out too quickly was that of holding the rudder. Becoming obvious the first few days, I could see that the kind of energy we were expending to rudder the raft was going to make us much too weak too early in the trip. We would have to do something about tying down the rudder. Unfortunately, neither Charlie nor I knew much about tying knots. Yes, we were in the Navy, but as aviators we were never required to tie knots.

We took the extra line that made up the sheet lines to the bottom of the sail, and tied them off to the end of the rudder. Looking closely at my photos, you will see the conglomeration of knots that we tied in order to keep the rudder in position without having the knots slip. Once at a boat show, I gave my survival talk, and showed these same pictures. Someone commented that the rudder line had a beautiful double bowline tied in it. If I tied a double bowline, it was purely accidental. I thought what I tied was a bunch of granny knots! When the knots slipped, I just tied some more knots. I kept tying knots until the rudder wouldn't slip anymore. I may have had a couple of sheepshanks, a bowline or two, and lord knows what else. I just tied knots until the rudder wouldn't slip, that's it.

Regardless of our self-imposed silence during the day to conserve energy, we did enjoy a little conversation after our evening meals, and also with our last drink of water for the day. We talked about where we had grown up, and how we happened to get into the Navy. Charlie asked me lots of questions about being married, and talked about his relationship with Nancy. I kidded Charlie that after being in this raft for two months, he would probably marry the first girl he found on the beach. As it happened, he did get married in Hawaii, and he did marry Nancy when she flew over to Hawaii to meet us.

George plotting the position using the Solargram. With a sunrise and sunset time and an accurate watch we could plot our position within about 30 nautical miles.

George splashing the soap off and just having a little fun. How often does one get to take a bath in the middle of the ocean?

Courageous as she looked from aft. The little net lying over the rudder is the net Charlie used in trying to catch fish.

George pulls himself to Courageous after his bath. The bath felt great but it took a lot of energy to get in and out of the little life raft.

George putting on his undershirt after a bath at sea. We took a bath after 35 days whether we needed it or not.

George stood up one time during the trip for this picture. This was not easy as it took a while to stand up on very weak legs. Our leg muscles were literally gone. Our bodies consumed the tissue we used the least, and that was in our legs.

Charlie on watch. We were so far out of shipping lanes that it really didn't make sense to waste energy sitting up looking around.

The steel leadered line seen on the left of the picture has George's tennis shoe on a large hook. The Great White's dorsal fin can be seen above the dark shape of the shark. When George saw this shark it was no more than a foot from his elbow.

Charlie holding two of the dorado he shot with the spear. After 54 days we finally had some real food.

George holding one of the dorado. Charlie had the job of shooting the fish, George the job of cleaning them.

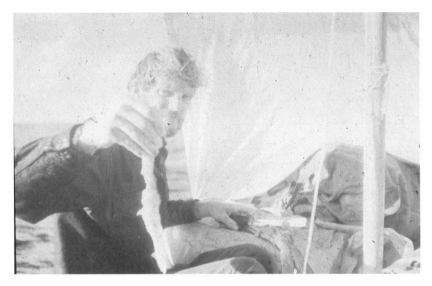

George offering Charlie some raw fish. This was not the first animal we caught, as we both caught birds by hand.

George talking on the UHF radio to the Coast Guard C-130 who was out looking for us. The pilot advised us that we were now "an official Navy project".

This is a picture taken from the Coast Guard C-130 aircraft of *Courageous* as we were about 200 miles from Hawaii. A small raft in a big ocean.

Charlie coming aboard the Coast Guard Cutter. The Navy had flown doctors to Hawaii and they wanted us picked up. The water Charlie is standing in was due to the fish biting a hole in the raft.

*And a gray mist on the sea's
face and a gray dawn breaking.*
—John Mansfield

VI

Our First Contact at Sea

After seven days of making little headway in near gale force winds, the wind died down to nothing. The condition of the sea followed suit in a few hours, calming somewhat. Now able to keep the sail up all day and all night, we reverted to our tiring four-hour watch routine. We would have to keep an alert vigilance since we were moving into the lower area of the California coast where shipping lanes would cross our path.

Dolphin appeared from time to time to keep us company. They were welcomed diversions to help pass the time of day. Thirst was our constant companion. Dehydration was absolutely the most uncomfortable condition to endure on the entire trip. I had assumed we would enjoy the beneficence of a Mother Nature rain at least sometime during the crossing. However it rained only once, and that was off the California coast, and "rain" is a misnomer to what was just heavy fog.

We each drank a little sea water mixed with our fresh water. The solar stills produced water, but because of the high overcast blocking the sun, we shared about 16 ounces a day. Personally, I thought the sea water gave the distilled water a much better taste, or at least some taste, because water from the solar still had a plastic and talcum powder taste.

Thankfully, the latter wore off after a few weeks, but those first few drinks from a solar still are not very tasty no matter how badly needed.

Of course we knew the ever potential danger in drinking sea water. Everyone has surely seen a movie, or read a book about the castaway who drinks sea water and goes mad. The human brain, in balance electro-chemically, loses its ability to function properly if certain substances disturb that electrolytic balance. The castaway who drinks pure sea water not only alters his brain's electrolytic balance, but significantly changes that balance in other organs of his body. But long before a person's brain functions deteriorate, that person is likely to get a severe case of diarrhea. And, of course, that additional loss of water coupled with the person drinking sea water will hasten the loss of brain function.

With the foregoing in mind, we determined to take precautions in drinking the small amounts of sea water that we had been adding to our distilled water. Charlie began to feel that he was having some lower intestinal discomfort, so he stopped mixing the sea water entirely. Medically, it was beyond our expertise to evaluate his symptoms as the onset of diarrhea. We concluded that his stomachache may simply have been the result of our drastically changed diet. I wasn't having any problems, so I continued to drink the sea water mix, but on a more limited basis. We could not afford to have a self-induced medical emergency, so we opted on the side of caution.

Thus we settled into a drinking routine which we were to follow for the entire trip. Many people, including myself, may have questioned why the water containers or cups packed in survival kits are marked out in ounces. I can now tell you exactly why. If there is limited water, and more than one person aboard the life raft, you can bet your life that each one will want to witness that he or she gets the same amount of water as the others, to the exact fraction of an ounce. Charlie and I divided the water in front of each other. The person dividing the water attempted to split the portions as evenly as possible, and the person waiting had first choice for whichever cup. I always tried to choose the one I thought had the most water, and Charlie did the same.

There are stories about castaways found dead of dehydration, but who had as much as a quart of water tied to their raft. When I went through Navy survival training, we were taught to, " conserve the water, drink small amounts, and save it." One unfortunate, dehydrated pilot took the advice to the ultimate limit. He saved all of his water before he died from dehydration.

The best water reservoir in the world has to be the human body. Very small amounts of water are used with the most efficiency. I usually drank every drop of water as soon as it was time to drink. On balance during the trip, we consumed an average of ten to twelve ounces of water a day, getting less at the start of the trip, but more as we neared Hawaii because of longer sunny days. But, during that first month, there wasn't very much water. If there were only six ounces to drink, I drank it all at once, and Charlie would sometimes save a couple of ounces for a midnight drink. I don't know how he withstood the thirst knowing that he had water to drink, and not drink it. I was jealous that he had the discipline to wait that long. Without exception, each night that he had his little midnight drink, I wished that I'd saved a little too. But, I was never able to save any.

On the morning of the seventh day I woke up to find us in "pea soup" fog. It was so thick I could cut it. On this particular morning, I was the early riser, in fact, I was always the early riser. Charlie liked to sleep later, but once the sun was up, so was I. Never was I one to just lie in bed all morning, even when I didn't have to work. A little breeze blew in from the northeast so I gathered in the sea anchors and lifted the sail. With the sail up, I noticed that drops of water condensed on the sail, slid down to the bottom, and became large drops pooling on the front of the boat. I yelled at Charlie to get up, so we could collect some of that precious water.

Charlie wasted no time in coming up on "deck". We spread out the tarp so that most of its surface area was exposed to the fog. We pulled in the bottom of the sail to form a kind of funnel. Then we placed a water bottle at the bottom of the funnel, and sat there for almost five hours collecting water from the heavy fog. It was beautiful. We let large drops form on the sail, then shook it gently. Drops of water slid down the sail to form larger and larger drops. In total, we collected about a quart and a half of water, and drank about a pint each as it collected. It was the best drink I'd ever had. And it picked up our spirits. We were like a couple of kids in a sand box as we watched the water run down the sail. We licked up every drop while the fog was thick, but as the fog dissipated, the water droplets trickled down to nothing.

About 10:30 that same morning, we lay back enjoying the calmer seas. We were moving along at about one knot, and had almost all of the sea water cleared out of the boat. With no idea of how long the fine weather would hold, we just took in the ocean and air with all our senses. I was at the helm, and Charlie sat leaning against the pontoon.

There was little wind, and the waves were nothing more than long swells. I began to hear a sound that was out of the ordinary. At first very faint, I couldn't make out its direction. I thought the sound was coming from our boat. Then I looked across the ocean to see if an animal was making the noise. The sound grew louder. Charlie and I both concluded that it was a mechanical sound and had to be coming from a boat or ship. Visibility was about five miles. If we could determine the direction of the peculiar sound, we might see what was out there with us.

"Smoke!" I yelled, pointing toward the eastern horizon. I could see a small column of smoke coming from below the horizon. It wasn't long before we could see just a speck of something under the smoke. The boat or ship looked as if it were coming almost directly toward us.

"It looks like a fishing boat, " Charlie commented.

"I think you're right, the engine sounds like one of those engines I remember those boats in Hong Kong harbor used, putt, putt, putt."

"You reckon we ought to signal it? It might give us a test of our flares." I speculated.

"Well if we signal it, then they'll think we're in trouble, and they might call the Coast Guard." Charlie replied.

"You're right! Besides, it looks like it's coming right at us anyway."

On the list of observations we planned to make on the expedition was the number of ships that would pass us without seeing us. Legendary are the claims of castaways who saw ships passing close by, but were never seen. Many waved clothing and yelled themselves hoarse only to remain invisible. Even their flares were not picked up by passing vessels, nor, as in one case, did it prevent their being run over!

There is good reason for that. First, many ships operate

in the open ocean without someone actually scanning the ocean. Such procedure is contrary to open sea navigation rules, but it does happen more than one might think. I've been on the bridge of a number of ships, and saw for myself that a proper watch is not always kept. Even on ships that have people standing visual watches it happens because of the fatigue factor in looking across miles of ocean for several hours. The sun, reflecting off the water, and onto white caps and swells, strains the eyes, and makes it almost impossible to see a small boat or raft on the water.

Even if the castaway activates a flare, the flare must compete with the sun's brightness and its diamond-like reflections on the water. A smoke flare in a wind above ten knots is almost useless because the smoke disperses so rapidly. The castaway's best chance to be seen by a ship is at night by using an aerial flare, or a bright, hand-held flare. Of course if no one is on the bridge looking out, the brightest flares in the world will do no good.

There have been castaways, however, who have employed unique ways to attract attention. A few were seen by simply splashing the water with their hands or an oar. One fellow who feared that a search helicopter would miss him, set his boat on fire! He took the last possible chance of being seen since it was late in the afternoon, and he thought he might be looking at that helicopter for the last time. The crewman on the 'copter saw the smoke, and credited the man's burning boat for saving his life.

There was no doubt about it, the boat was indeed coming toward us. It was about sixty feet long, and definitely a commercial fishing boat. We could make out someone in the wheelhouse. There didn't seem a whole lot to do but wave as the boat neared. When the boat came to within thirty feet of us, it came to a halt. A man in the pilot house yelled, "What are you guys doing out here? Are you in trouble?"

I yelled back, "No, we're okay." Before I could finish my statement, he asked if we knew how far out to sea we were.

"I'm guessing about a hundred miles," I answered.

"Do you have a motor?" he questioned.

"No, we're on an expedition to Hawaii," I answered.

"You're going to Hawaii in a rubber boat. Are you kidding? " he asked.

I tried to explain what we were doing. He called for

someone below decks.

"How many of you are on board?" I asked.

"Just two of us, me and my wife."

He yelled again for his wife who was below deck. She came up and waved at us as he explained to her that we were going to Hawaii. We advised what we were about, and they finally believed us. He went into the pilothouse to get a camera, and took our picture. His wife had gone down below, and reappeared with a beautiful fish that looked to weigh about ten pounds. Because we told them what we'd been eating, and planned on catching fish, she considered that it wouldn't be cheating if we were given a raw fish. But, no thanks, we considered it to be cheating. Turning down that fish was hard to do because we were both getting a little hungry. We thanked them for the offer. Then they offered a drink, but now that we had some water we assumed we'd be getting even more from Mother Nature later on. That assumption was going to prove false.

They were out of Morrow Bay heading to Alaska for the fishing season. They confirmed our position as not too far from that of our estimate. They bid us good luck, and motored away to the north. As they pulled away from us we could see the name of their boat was the, "Millie G". We never looked up the "Millie G" after the trip, but I wish I'd had done so; a copy of the picture they took would have rounded out our memorabilia.

I need to mention a couple of important bits of information that concerned our bodies, or things a castaway could expect to undergo. I mentioned Dougal Robertson's amazing survival feat earlier. Mrs. Robertson, his wife, was a nurse and very concerned for the health of her family in the lifeboat. Because they were not having bowel movements, she worried about constipation, so attempted to give them enemas. Because all of us are accustomed to having regular bowel movements, their absence causes a minor concern, at least in normal conditions. But when one is taking in very little food, all of that food may be absorbed by the body leaving little to be evacuated from the intestine. I reminded myself of this, because as Dr. Bombard observed, people can worry themselves into a mental state, a threat more dangerous to their health than the problem they are worrying about. Charlie had two small bowel movements, and I had one during our 56 day trip. All three occurred in the first week of the trip. For fifty days after, neither of us had another bowel movement. Our bodies were not only consuming all the food we took in, but fat and muscle were absorbed as nourishment to vital organs.

Our urine began to get much darker than was normal, and we seemed to urinate about the same amount of water that we ingested. We were eating the sucrose candy, which may have accounted for the production of that much urine. As the trip bore on, the urine continued to darken, and become heavier. The volume, however, always seemed to equal that which we took in. The heavy, dark urine worried us somewhat because we couldn't shake the doctors' prediction that we could indeed suffer permanent kidney damage.

We had looked into health insurance before the trip, but no insurance company wanted anything to do with us. The prospect of becoming permanently disabled bothered me more than anything, both before and during the trip. Neither of us had much money, certainly not an amount to cover a permanent disabling condition. We each knew we were jeopardizing our flying careers, either for the Navy, or for future airline jobs. We both loved to fly, and we hated the prospect that a disability would prevent our flying, especially since it was our livelihood prior to the trip.

Next, we were concerned about our eyes because of the constant exposure to the glare off the ocean. I had enough trouble passing an eye test without piling on additional complications. We had countered that potential problem by purchasing good sunglasses for the trip. Speaking of glare, castaways are known to have suffered, "snow blindness" from long over-exposure to glare on the open ocean and its reflective light.

The "Millie G" turned out to be the only boat or ship that saw us during the entire trip. We spotted a couple of other ships later in the trip, one was at night, and the other an air craft carrier as we neared Hawaii. We gave many a thought for the remainder of the trip, to the "Millie G" and the fish that was offered. I still picture the lady from the "Millie G", holding that fish by the tail, offering it to us. Weeks after turning down the offer, we still debated whether or not acceptance of the fish would have been cheating. After all, it was a raw fish, not a cooked fish, and besides, we were obviously going to catch lots of fish anyway. One more would not have mattered.

And all I ask is a tall ship and a star to steer her by,
—John Mansfield

VII

Continuing South

The wind continued to blow from the northwest, and we continued to sail almost due south. We were now sailing twenty-four hours a day, and making about two to two and a half knots per hour. With the steadiness of our present progress, we established a routine that seemed to add some order to our lives, beginning with regular meals at precise times. Breakfast was 8 AM, lunch at 12:00, and dinner at 5 PM. When meal-time approached we broke out the candy jar, and each took a piece of candy. The Charms candies we had elected to carry were packaged in bags of approximately fifteen separate candies of four or five different flavors ranging from cherry, grape, grapefruit, strawberry, etc. Before each meal we picked out our favorite flavor of candy, talked a little, and kept our eyes on our watches. When the second hand of the watch crossed, "twelve", we popped that one piece of candy into our mouths. As the days worn on we found that we each had our favorite flavor of candy. However, it soon became apparent that neither of us liked the grapefruit, so we began to have a surplus of grapefruit.

Then a very interesting thing happened to us, our taste buds went blind. Curiously, the loss of a sense of taste set in after a couple of weeks. We could detect the taste of salt, but it was difficult to taste the candy's flavor. We could tell it was sweet, but that was all. This became a blessing in disguise so we made up a game. I was the first to realize that I couldn't really tell what flavor I was sucking on. In fact I had to take the candy out of my mouth to check the flavor, by the color of the candy. Cherry was red, grape was purple, grapefruit was white, etc. One morning I bet Charlie that he couldn't tell what breakfast flavor he had in his mouth if he didn't see it. He thought he could, so I picked out a piece of candy, grapefruit of course, and without Charlie seeing it, had him close his eyes and open his mouth. I popped the candy into his mouth, and he sucked on it for a couple of minutes. He guessed it was cherry, and didn't believe me when I told him it was not, so he took it out of his mouth to check. When Charlie saw the candy was grapefruit, he screwed up his mouth as if all of a sudden it tasted terrible.

We played our eating game so long as the candy lasted. It was a good way to get rid of the grapefruit, and provided some amusement. Amazing to us was how much our sense of sight affected our sense of taste. If we saw the candy, we could taste the flavor. I could suck on a candy that I hadn't seen, and not taste anything but its sweetness. As soon as I took the candy out of my mouth and saw its color, the flavor would come immediately. The food game was lots of fun, and we had some good laughs, always when we gave the other guy the grapefruit, which was often.

Once we had eaten, we settled into what was to become our daily routine. The person at the helm watched the compass, and steered as closely west as the wind would allow. However, we were finding it impossible to make any progress to the west, which became somewhat discouraging. The person giving up the helm pulled the tarp over himself, and either sat and rested, or slept.

I began to notice small pilot fish between the two pontoons. Pilot fish usually follow larger scavengers like shark to eat the shark's leftovers. The Zodiac's attraction for the pilot fish were the small barnacles under the boat giving us the look of a big fish, so they stuck with us. I watched one for hours. He was no more than three or four inches under the surface of the water, and I began to regard him as food. He would swim under the boat then reappear again between the pontoons. I named him, Henry. Henry was about three inches long and very slim. When I made a couple of grabs for him, he was too quick for me, and swam away.

At noon, when we took our lunch, we would take our first drink of water for the day. By lunch time the solar still had usually made some water, hopefully anticipated for our meal. We would then change the watch and positions. I did most of the navigating, and at sometime during the day, would plot our estimated position. Many days I couldn't get a fix with the Solargram, so I would plot a "DR" (Dead Reckoning) position using compass heading and estimated speed.

Since I was the early riser, part of my duties as navigator entailed the recording of sunrise and sunset times. Navigating with the Solargram required an accurate time of both. On many days I could record only an accurate sunrise, as clouds would block the sunset, or vice versa. Generally, my navigation came out fairly accurate, however, I managed to make a very fundamental error in my navigation calculations, which caused us some problems.

All of my training in navigation consisted of plotting a course of intended flight on an aviation chart. Some charts are oriented to true north, and others to magnetic north. The magnetic pole can vary from the true North Pole by twenty degrees, an error that requires recalibration and publication of new charts as it slowly changes position. The chart we used was oriented to true north. In the life raft we followed a compass heading first, and then plotted a DR position. In aviation, we plot a true course, and then apply magnetic variation to the true course in order to arrive at a compass heading. In the life raft, the opposite rule applied. It had been years since Charlie and I had plotted a course on a chart, an elementary form of navigation, since modern aircraft are loaded with all forms of electronic navigation, course selectors, corrections, etc. We did remember one old navigation adage, "East is least and West is best," meaning that easterly variation must be subtracted from the true heading, and added if westerly. Marine and aviation charts clearly depict degrees of variation, so there remains little guesswork involved in making corrections. Right!

Unfortunately, after we started out I couldn't remember whether the saying applied to compass heading or true heading for plotting our course. As an example, if my compass heading read 235 degrees, I was applying magnetic correction in the wrong direction. The variation on most of our trip averaged about 14 degrees East, and I was thinking that I needed to subtract 14 degrees from our compass heading in order to obtain true heading for plotting on the chart. What I should have done was add the Easterly variation to compass heading. So in my error of plotting our compass heading of 235 degrees, I subtracted 14 degrees, arriving at a mistaken true heading of 221 degrees instead of the correct heading of 249 degrees.

I didn't realize my error until 30 days into the trip. Because of my math, or lack of it, I estimated that we were a lot farther south than our actual position. My "DR" position, after 30 days, put me almost 200 miles farther south than what the Solargram showed. I suspected for awhile that it was the southern current, or Japanese Current, as it is commonly called, that was carrying us much farther and faster to the south than either of us expected. It wasn't until August 4th, a month into the trip, that I realized what I had been doing. On that day I got a really good fix with the Solargram showing us about 200 miles north of my "DR" fix. It was then I suspected something was wrong. We discussed the possible cause of the error, and it was Charlie who finally realized what I had been doing wrong. It was a foolish mistake, and I later ensured against the possibility of someone else doing the same by including in the Solargram, instructions and examples of magnetic application.

My intent had been to sail south to 21 degrees north latitude, then sail that line of latitude until we reached Hawaii. By sailing the 21st parallel we would intercept the Hawaiian Islands in about the middle of the chain, or in the vicinity of Maui. We calculated that if we shot for Maui, and missed it either to the north or south, we would reach at least one of the islands. My "DR" position on August 2nd, showed us already below the 21st parallel. In my concern that we might drift further south, I opted to hold a steady northwesterly heading to sail back up to 21 degrees latitude. And this was the point where it would have been a bit of luck to discover that we were actually above 24 degrees, and should have continued to sail south. But I went on correcting to the north when I should have been sailing south! Dumb, dumb, dumb.

By the time I realized my mistake, and replotted all the headings, I found that my "DR" position differed by roughly 40 miles from the position indicated on the Solargram. We were 1260 miles from Hawaii by the time I realized the error, so we had to correct our position by over 180 miles to the south. That isn't a big problem for a sailboat, but we were now entering the trade winds which were forcing us almost due west. If we didn't intercept the 21st parallel before thirty days passed, we could sail right past Hawaii to the north.

In navigating with the Solargram, or in using the North Star or Southern Cross as a guide, a castaway should do everything possible to reach the predetermined latitude well to the east or west of his destination. The reason for this is the difficulty in determining longitude. With no watch or chronometer for determining longitude, it is impossible to sail a direct line to your destination. If a castaway does try to sail direct, he could miss his intended point of landing, and would never know whether he was east or west of his destination. This wouldn't make a big difference if he were attempting to intercept a large continent, but in trying to intercept small islands, the error could be deadly. My emphatic recommendation is for sailing to the intended latitude as soon as possible, well out from the intended destination. This will positively prove the surest way to the destination.

I have often been asked if, after having sailed and lived with my survival kit for two months, would I make any changes to it. I usually answer, "not a thing." All worked pretty much as I claimed it would. But I do usually forget to tell people how dumb I was for making that simple math error, and made sure no one else would do the same. Nowadays, the one piece of equipment that I would pack in lieu of a solar still is the reverse osmosis machine for water-making. However, the machine has only become available in the last fifteen years.

Also, if one had a hand held GPS, that would be of great benefit as a direct heading could be plotted. Again, however, in a rubber boat with no keel, if one were to sail directly to an island and miss it on the down wind side, it would be impossible to sail back up wind to the island.

Chewing the food of sweet and bitter fancy.
—Shakespeare

VIII

Daily Routine

Our daily routine was becoming rather boring, yet we still kept a modified watch schedule. Someone had to stay awake, more or less all night, so we could keep the boat on course. Once we finally encountered the publicized steady "Force 4" wind, we found that the boat would stay on course for hours with no help from us. We simply tied down the rudder, trimmed the sail, and the boat held course nicely so long as the wind did not change.

As usual, I got up first to check the sun. It was always a little bit exciting to see a beautiful sunrise. When we had breakfasted, and tended the solar stills, our morning chores were done. If there was water in the boat, we would try to dry it out a bit. I hated the water running into my ears at night, and that's what happened if my head dropped too low to the floor while asleep. We were wet and cold most of the time, at least for the first 30 days.

At noon we had our lunch, drained what fresh water we might have in the solar still, and had our first drink of the day. We talked some, but mostly just rested. At six o'clock we had supper, another drink, and waited for sunset. In the twilight, I would plot a fix, and we would usually have a small talk centered on our present location. For days, the trip was just that boring. But we wanted it to be boring. We wanted to save every bit of energy we had. Often the conservation of energy becomes confused with the good intentions to keep mind and body occupied for morale purposes.

There are accounts of castaways who, under the strong rule of a senior officer, were kept busy doing silly chores that consumed energy. I would venture to say that the officers kept their charges busy with the good intention of keeping their minds off the horrible death they might be destined to suffer. On the other hand, we knew where we were going, and we had a plan for survival. We did not need to waste any more energy than necessary, nor waste time with thoughts of dying. We thought positively.

Henry stayed with us day after day. Finally, it became too much for Charlie to bear. For the first five days of the trip, we felt a kind of hunger. I mean hunger that comes with pains in the stomach. But after that first week of little food, we no longer had physical pain from hunger, we just became weaker, and couldn't blot food from our minds. Charlie was at the helm one morning and decided that he could catch Henry in the net of a hammock we devised for keeping supplies. He worked himself around to face aft, and leaned over the stern while trying to "net" Henry. He worked for about an hour and a half trying to catch Henry. I got a good laugh at Charlie, burning more calories than he could afford to lose. Even if he caught Henry, the calories he gained by eating him wouldn't replace the calories he had burned in trying to catch him.

Nevertheless, I had to admire Charlie's persistence. It was already July 14th, and we were beginning to get extremely hungry. We still had no physical discomfort, but we couldn't get food off our minds. During the day we talked about the different foods we enjoyed, including our favorite, "mother's recipes," and what we ourselves enjoyed cooking. Even our dreams at night became interlaced with dreams of food. This "food craving" state of mind remained with us the entire trip.

The most interesting biological effect of starving, at least to us, was its lack of physical pain. We felt weak, but our stomachs, intestines, mouths, throats, etc. did not cause any discomfort. In fact, since experiencing our kind of starvation, I often tell people that starving to death would certainly not be the most unpleasant way to die. After fifty-six days at sea and having little food, my weight dropped from 186 to 128 pounds.

At the end of our expedition, I could easily imagine my lying down in the weak condition I was in, going to sleep, and never waking up. Since then, when I see pictures of starving people such as those in Somali or Ruwanda, I think of how terrible and awful it is that people still starve on this earth. But I am comforted to apply my own experience in thinking that their emaciated physical appearance was not accompanied by equally unbearable physical pain.

No matter how laughable Charlie's efforts to catch Henry, he inspired me to get out the fishing kit. I took out a silver lure and attached a plastic worm to the hook. I thought the silver lure, spinning in the clear water with the sun reflecting off it, and the worm wiggling behind the lure would surely attract a fish. I messed with that setup all day, and never so much as got a bite, so I just left the line and lure in the water hoping a fish might take the bait sooner or later.

Something we both enjoyed doing that didn't take much energy was making up a recipe book. Since we couldn't get our minds off food, we took out paper and pen to write down delicious-sounding recipes that we would like to try when we reached land. Talk about torture! In some subliminal reaches of his mind, mounds of pancakes became Charlie's fantasy. He raved about huge plates of steaming pancakes smothered with melted butter, real butter, dripping down the sides, and covered with real maple syrup. My favorite recipe was sea-soned ground beef with jalapeno peppers, onions and mush-rooms sliced and sautéed with the beef, then smothered with parmesan cheese melted over the beef and vegetables until it permeated the entire mix. I thought about that dish a lot on the trip. Oddly, I had never cooked or eaten that dish in my life, nor did I do so back on land. But Charlie's pancakes made the bigger impression; we ate a heck of a lot of pancakes after we landed in Hawaii.

Although we lost a lot of equipment after turning over, we still had our stethoscope, thermometer, and blood pressure cuff for taking vital signs. We didn't get it out very often due to the effort it took and the fact that we didn't want to get it wet. It was a pain in the butt to go forward to get into the boxes that contained the medical equipment and the two-way radios. If it happened to be a relatively calm day, with no water splashing into the boat, we would get out the radios and medical equipment. So, from time to time we took our temperature, and checked our blood pressure, but didn't do it often by any means.

One day there was a large group of dolphin swimming along with us. We weren't opposed to eating dolphin, but they swam too far away for a good shot with the spear. It was nice having their company, and fun to watch them. Curious creatures, they were probably drawn to the shadow of our boat. I'm sure we didn't present much of a challenge to them speed wise as we moved so slowly, and they soon bored and swam away toward the south.

A few chapters back I discussed our excretory problems; that we had urinated into a plastic bottle because it was easier and safer than trying to hang over the side, especially at night. One incident occurred pertaining to our "pee" bottle, and our water bottles. We still laugh about it, but it was not so funny at the time. One evening Charlie was dividing the water, and handed me my water bottle. I drank it right down, and immediately knew something was wrong.

"That tasted salty," I said, looking at Charlie for some explanation.

One look at Charlie's face, and I knew what he had done. He had put my water ration in the urine. Since we'd lost a good deal of our sense of taste, all I actually had tasted was somewhat salty water. It bothered Charlie more than me that he'd given me the wrong bottle. Later when we talked about it, Charlie admitted to thinking his error might have been an indication that we were losing some mental capacity. Hell, if we'd had any mental capacity in the first place we wouldn't have been out there! It was just a silly mistake, and we had some good laughs about it back on land. As a future precaution however, I cut some grooves in the top of the urine bottle so we could tell by the feel, especially in darkness, whether or not we had our hands on the urine bottle.

At night we enjoyed watching the stars. It was so incredibly clear and beautiful that we lay on top of the tarp, and watched the sky for hours. Charlie knew the names of many of the stars and constellations, imparting his substantial knowledge of astronomy on our way to Hawaii. We enjoyed these talks at night. And so we settled into our new routine. Even though we were hundreds of miles at sea in an inflatable boat, we had become so accustomed to, and comfortable with the surroundings that we no longer gave a conscious thought to the fragility of our position, that is, until one night about 300 miles southwest of Los Angeles, the tranquil spell was broken.

It was about 10:00 at night, and I was at the helm. The weather was good, and the wind blew from the northwest at about ten knots. It was beautiful sailing weather with nothing to do but enjoy the night. I looked around every now and then to make sure there were no ships bearing down on us for we were in an area of some heavily traveled shipping lanes, and our visibility to the horizon was only three miles. It wouldn't take long for a ship traveling at twenty-five knots to appear over the horizon, and be on top of us. To say the least, we had limited ability to clear the way from anything very quickly.

The moon was out, shimmering across the miles and miles of endless water. Charlie was resting under the tarp. It would be his watch in a couple of hours. I was staring to the west when all of a sudden something came out of the water not more than ten feet away. My first thought was of a submarine surfacing. There was a tremendous blow, and the air filled with a fishy-smelling mist. It was a whale! I could make out its head, and its barnacle-covered back. It broke through the surface, and slammed back under with its huge tail flipping the air to make a whopping splash. Visions of Moby Dick popped in my head as I saw the power in that tail. It could so easily crush us.

"Charlie!" I yelled. "Whale to starboard!"

Charlie damned near killed himself getting out from under the tarp. We were in the veritable center of a school of whales. It was fascinating, but extremely scary. We were helpless to do anything but watch. I never knew that whales had so many barnacles attached to their backs. I asked Charlie if whales could recognize, or even cared about what might be above them. They were so close I was concerned that one would come up from under, and flip us over. Yet I wasn't so worried about flipping over as I was about its barnacles ripping the boat apart. When I cut my feet on the barnacles attached to our underbelly the day we turned over, I learned how razor sharp they are. There was little doubt in my mind that we would be in a very bad situation if one of the whales ran into us.

We counted five to six whales in the school. They were traveling south, and seemed content to cruise along with us for awhile. It was wondrously fascinating to see those large animals in their natural beauty. They surfaced all around us, on both starboard and port sides. We couldn't tell where they were until they broke the surface. I kept looking behind, thinking I would see one ready to surface right under the boat, but they kept their distance. The scene was indescribable; to see an animal so huge emerge out of the jet black sea, and so close by. One of them surfaced just to our starboard beam about seven feet away. I watched its back come out of the water as it blew air from its spout, and saw that its tail was about to slam down very near the boat with a power that was awesome. Even a gentle slap could have done irreparable damage to *Courageous*, not to mention us! Somehow I didn't relish the idea of being in the water with a bunch of whales. Their tails rose up to tower over us then slid beneath the surface with a splash, spraying water for at least twenty to thirty feet.

Our encounter with the whales lasted less than five minutes, but every minute was terrifying. They drew from us such mixed emotions. Even though we may have been in mortal danger, we couldn't help admire their beauty, grace and majesty. It was an experience I will never forget. Had it occurred during the day, the display may not have concerned us so much, but at night, their whereabouts in relation to the raft was more than disconcerting. It was to be our first and last encounter with whales.

There is an old Navy saying about flying off aircraft carriers; it goes something like this, "hours and hours of boredom punctuated by seconds of terror." That's how we were contemplating this trip, days and days of boredom filled with hours of terror. We sat, or rather lay, in the raft doing nothing almost all day every day. We didn't want to do anything that would use our zealously guarded energy. We tried to cut out any extraneous motion that would deplete our already conserved body energy. Besides, after a couple of weeks of starvation we didn't have the energy to lift the proverbial feather. Aside from that, we felt there would be a few more occasions when we would have to call upon what reserve energy we had stored, in particular, we suspected there would be other storms. We began to feel ourselves fortunate that we had turned the raft over on the second day out. Primarily, having had the energy to get it back upright, and secondly, in learning to take down the sail when the wind and waves became dangerous.

We had already become gun shy about storms after that second day. With the amount of energy we were left with, we'd never have the energy to helm the raft if we encountered another storm such as the one we weathered. Then again, if we kept the sail down too long, it would take much longer to get to Hawaii than I planned. I hoped the data on the pilot charts was accurate, and that we would have many balmy sailing days in the westerly-flowing trade winds.

It was not until July 19th that we finally began to sail westward. Up until that time the wind had been varying from north-east to north-west, continually blowing us south. At times we were actually sailing south-east, back toward the coast. We were hundreds of miles at sea only because the coast of Mexico falls so sharply east. I made a joke, regretting it for fear it could come true, that it looked like we were going to end up in Acapulco instead of Hawaii. We had some good laughs about the surprise to Judi and Nancy if they got a call from Acapulco in lieu of Hawaii!

The further south we sailed, the longer the trip would be. All we could do was laugh about how far south we'd come. Incredibly, we were almost twelve-hundred miles due west of Mazatlan when we finally caught the westerly trade winds. As evidenced when I plotted it out, we obviously hadn't sailed a straight course, but not that we had expected to be able to do that in the turbulent weather we had been through earlier. If, by design, we could have been dispatched a couple of hundreds of miles further to the west at the start, we would have had earlier and more favorable help, current-wise and wind-wise, in intercepting a westerly course.

Nevertheless, the problems of the first couple of weeks made our expedition more realistic, and more in line with the probable events that a castaway would encounter. I've always espoused the philosophy that a sailor or aviator is by nature independent in his sailing or flying, a fact that preordains his independence in methods of survival. An aviator has an advantage over a sailor, because he is bound by law to file a flight plan in order to fly across the ocean. He must have onboard the equipment to maintain radio communication with an Oceanic Air Traffic Control Center. If he has an emergency, as I did in 1984, in losing the engine and ditching an airplane 600 miles south of Hawaii, the aviator can radio for help.

Most sailors on the other hand, do not file float plans, and they don't give regular position reports. Their usual mode of operation involves nothing more than telling a friend or relative that they will call when they arrive at their destination. That could be a week or two months. If trouble develops, they're likely to be at sea a long time before anyone even misses them. By the time they are reported missing, there is little chance that the Coast Guard or anyone else will launch a rescue effort. The Coast Guard can't search an entire ocean if the sailor left no clue to his intended course or his estimated time of arrival at destination. Most world cruising sailors with whom I've talked, would say that they don't give regular position reports.

Consequently, the sailor, and to a limited extent the aviator, are independent in their sailing or flying, and they must be independent in their means of survival, or have the ability to save themselves. For a sailor, a big part of saving himself is in having the ability to maneuver a life boat or raft, and sail it to safety. Unfortunately, the nearest point of land is not always the most viable point of land. That reality became apparent the first week of our trip. Very possibly Charlie and I could have sailed back to the coast of California or Mexico. But once we were south of Los Angeles, it is doubtful that we could have made landfall anywhere to the east. We would have encountered westerly currents eventually, and would have found it impossible to sail to the east.

Recalling the many stories of my research, one in particular stands out. A group of young people were sailing a trimaran from the Pacific Northwest down along the coast towards San Francisco, when their boat overturned in heavy seas about forty miles west of Eureka, California. They were fortunate in that most multi-hull boats do not tend to sink because the hulls are made watertight, and they do not have the heavy ballast as does a conventional sailboat. But even though the boat stayed afloat, there was no hope of getting her upright. These people had neither raft nor lifeboat to sail the moderately short distance back to the coast. After weeks and weeks at sea, the boat was finally sighted by a passing freighter about midway between San Francisco and Hawaii. Sadly, only one person survived the ordeal even though they had food and water stored in the overturned boat.

Consequently, Charlie and I were ourselves in a kind of

situation that a castaway might find himself if he were to be adrift off the west coast of California, i.e., we were forced to sail west to Hawaii in order to sail to the most viable point of land. It would have been virtually impossible to sail or paddle an inflatable boat back to the West Coast. After playing around with inflatable boats and life rafts for twelve years, I came to realize how difficult it is to paddle against wind and current. In fact, it is totally impossible to paddle an inflatable, round life raft against even the lightest wind or current. After Charlie and I returned home to start our survival business, we tried, under the most controlled conditions, to paddle a life raft against a light wind and current, but had no success. Life raft manufacturers are still packing paddles into life rafts though, I suppose it's for the reason that unthinking persons expect to see paddles in a boat. Believe me, the space those paddles take up could be far better used for something that would do the castaway some good. I tried for years to get raft manufacturers to change paddles for something useful with absolutely no success.

We tried to keep a record of events on a day-to-day basis. Usually there wasn't much to log except the time of sunrise or sunset. Some days we might have seen a bird, or a couple of times at night, seen the lights of a far away ship. On the evening of July 14th, we saw the lights of a high flying aircraft heading west presumably out of LA. We figured it was headed for Hawaii so we got the radio out and tried to make contact. We used the VHF radio on the emergency channel, 121.5 mHz. We weren't too certain how we wanted to make the call, so we just broadcast in the blind the following:

"Any aircraft, any aircraft, this is *Courageous* calling on 121.5, over."

Since we'd had the forethought to write letters telling of our proposed trip to the corporate offices of all scheduled air carriers that flew to Hawaii, we hoped our call wouldn't be totally unexpected. This night we didn't have to wait long for an answer, for not one, but a couple of airliners responded. A Northwest flight, evidently closer, came in much clearer than the other aircraft. The pilot responded:

"*Courageous* this is Northwest 205 on 121.5, go ahead. Over."

"Northwest 205 this is the raft, *Courageous*. Could you switch to 123.4? Over."

"*Courageous*, Northwest 205, are you in difficulty? Over."

"Negative, Northwest. We are a life raft on a survival expedition to Hawaii. Over."

"*Courageous*, Northwest 205 switching to 123.4. Over"

"Roger, *Courageous* switching."

We had to make initial contact on 121.5, the emergency frequency, but we did not want to continue on that frequency in case someone might have an emergency and need to use it. We only had the two frequencies, emergency and 123.4 that we could use. The communications frequency, 123.4, is a frequency that some airliners use to relay messages to each other on the crossing to Hawaii, otherwise it isn't used much.

"Northwest 205, this is *Courageous* how do you read? Over."

"*Courageous*, Northwest 205 has you loud and clear. Now tell us once again who you are, and give us your position. Over."

"Northwest, *Courageous* is a life raft out of San Francisco bound for Hawaii. We departed San Francisco on July 4th, and estimate our position to be 33 degrees 45 minutes north, 122 degrees 30 minutes west. How copy? Over?"

"Good copy, *Courageous*. How many of you are there? Over."

"We are two navy pilots on a survival expedition. We are testing a survival kit, and hope to be in Hawaii in about six weeks. Are you bound for Hawaii? Over."

"That's affirmative, *Courageous*. We should be there in just over four hours. Over."

"Northwest, if you could call a number collect in San Francisco to let my wife know how we're doing we would appreciate it. Over."

"Ready to copy, *Courageous*. Go ahead. Over. "

"Please call area code 714-567-8989; this will reach my wife, Judi Sigler. She will notify the Coast Guard of our condition and position. We really appreciate your effort. Please call collect. She is expecting to hear from us. Thanks. Over."

"Copied, *Courageous*. Could you give us your names? Over."

"Roger that. First name George, Golf, Echo, Oscar, Romeo, Golf, Echo. Last name Sigler, Sierra, India, Golf, Lima, Echo, Romeo, and Charles Gore, Charlie, Hotel, Alpha, Romeo, Lima, Echo, Sierra; last name, Golf, Oscar, Romeo,

Echo. How copy? Over."

"Got it all, *Courageous*. Anything else we can do for you? Over."

"Well you could pass us down one of those first class dinners. We haven't eaten in a 10 days or so. Over."

"We would be glad to do that, but the girls haven't cooked yet, we'll catch you next time."

"Roger that, Northwest. Thanks for the help. *Courageous*, out."

"Northwest, out. Good luck."

We purposely did not mention that we had turned over, because we didn't want the Coast Guard coming out looking for us, and we didn't see the need to worry friends and relatives unnecessarily. Things were going OK now. We wished we were making better progress to the west, but on the whole felt we finally had things under control.

Contact with Northwest gave us a boost in spirits. It was a good test of our radio, and we felt a little more secure knowing that the radio worked. With a limited amount of battery time, we had to be careful to keep radio contacts as brief as possible. The radio was there for emergencies first, positions and conditions after. It was great, however, to talk with someone, and to know that Judi and Nancy would receive word that we were alive and well.

That night Charlie and I carried on somewhat of an imaginative conversation. We returned to the same subject that dominated our thoughts: what were they serving for dinner in first class on Northwest? I fantasized a starter of shrimp, brie cheese and champagne; an entree of prime rib roast of beef with a baked potato slathered with bacon, sour cream, etc.

Mmmmmm. Once again food dominated our thoughts and talk!

While on the subject of appetite, this is probably an appropriate time to bring up a delicate subject involving appetite, one that I'm sometimes asked about when recounting our journey. Aside from a lack of food for ten days or so, and in a weakened state, we were also two young, healthy males who would normally be thinking about sex. Fortunate for us, we never had a desire for, or even had that many thoughts of sex. We never got "horny", masturbated, or had "wet dreams". Once the body has been deprived of nutrients, the hormone level, especially testosterone, drops and the desire for sex is just not there. When Judi and Nancy met us in Hawaii, they had perfectly healthy, normal desires, and wanted to make love, but Charlie and I couldn't respond very well. We tried, but things just wouldn't turn up for us. Embarrassing evidence of low hormones! I had no desire or drive for sex for at least a week after getting to Hawaii.

Interestingly, when we talked about Nancy and Judi, we didn't talk about sex, we talked about taking them to our favorite Mexican restaurant, or about getting together to have a huge meal. We practically salivated at the thought of getting together to prepare a great seven-course meal for Nancy and Judi. No talk about sex with a woman, just food! It was an astonishing change of conversation for a couple of navy pilots, and far different from any we had in VietNam.

*They that go down to the sea in ships: and occupy
their business in great waters;
These men see the works of the Lord: and his
wonders in the deep.*
—Psalms cvii:23

IX

Moving West in the Trade Winds

It was not until July 19th, that the prevailing winds shifted noticeably toward the west. We had now entered the Trade Wind Belt, and would have steady west-flowing winds for the remainder of the trip, at least that's what the Pilot Charts depicted. We were at last well clear of major shipping lanes, and there was little reason to stand watch except to keep track of headings. We had become adept at trimming the sail to give us intended headings, and we wouldn't have to hold rudder, because we tied it mid-ship and left it there.

The weather was becoming much warmer, especially during the day. We rigged the tarp over us so that we could sit in the open and not get baked by the sun. We still water-soaked our clothing during the day to keep from sweating. The solar stills were making more water, but a high overcast of clouds kept them from producing as much water as we had hoped for. We were now making a little less than six ounces each from the stills, and supplementing it with what we had trapped in the heavy fog.

There were a few low clouds from time to time, but no rain. We saw rain falling from some of the clouds, but couldn't get to them in time. Once we saw a pretty good shower about a mile off to our left, and when we changed tack trying to get there, the upper level winds carried the clouds away faster than we could sail. Henry was still with us, but Charlie had given up trying to catch him. I still trolled bait, but neither he nor anything else seemed interested.

I removed my underwear from my feet during the day, and lay back with my feet drying in the sun. This helped the sores to dry up, and they began to heal enough where they didn't keep me awake at night. Our watch schedule was nothing more than a formality now. The person topside slept about as much as the person under the tarp. It was still cold at night, so we were careful to dry out as much as possible before nightfall.

On the evening of July 21st, the wind began to pickup. We had been enjoying a steady sixteen-knot wind for a number of days, but as the night wore on, the wind increased to a steady twenty-five knots with higher gusts. We had learned from experience that higher seas followed higher winds by about three hours, and the oncoming wind could make the seas quite rough, even rough enough to be dangerous.

I was at the helm when the seas eventually reached the point where I thought we ought to take down the sail. Then a large wave caught the boat on its starboard side, and lifted it out of the water. Even though Charlie was resting under the tarp he felt the jolt. Both he and I jumped to starboard to bring it back down. That ended it for sailing. We took down the sail, and put out the sea anchors. Excepting the upset on our first week, every time we encountered bad weather it was at night.

Once again waves crashed into the boat, and flooded us with water. It was impossible to keep anything dry. There was no respite but to crawl under the tarp and try to keep warm. We merely lay there and listened for the next wave. Certain of those waves made sounds that "told" us they were going to crash against the boat and give us a good soaking. I did a whole bunch of cussing these nights, but it didn't make one bit of difference. We crawled out every now and then to check on the stills, and to secure the sea anchors. We were to encounter three more of these storms at sea, but had learned to handle them with little trouble. Routinely, if the wind died down to twenty knots we sailed, but we had to untie the rudder in heavier seas to better control the boat.

I'll never forget how tired I was when I held that rudder for four hours. Our last major storm was on August 15th, and almost killed us with the effort it took to rudder the boat. In no way could we afford the amount of extra energy needed to hold rudder, but the alternative would have been to stop, and put out the sea anchors. Therefore, we ruddered. It was plainly miserable to sit out in the cold of night to hold that rudder! And there was just no way to keep warm. I slid down in the raft as low as I could to keep some wind off, and to keep the salt spray from soaking me. Of course I was already soaked, but my body heat had warmed the soaked wool clothing next to my skin, and I didn't relish each new soaking with the cold, ocean water.

On July 21st, the wind died. To warrant a description, a doldrum. There was not a breath of air on that part of the Pacific Ocean. It was the calmest sea I had ever seen. The sail hung limp on the mast, and for miles around us there was stillness, no water splashing against the boat, no wind to chill us. Though welcoming a break in the action, we were aware that the doldrums could add unwanted days, perhaps weeks to our trip.

The weather gave us an opportunity to dry out the boat, and dry out our sleeping bag. We no doubt had become inured to the odor in the boat; everything must have stunk to high heaven. It was a real pleasure to dry out. We hadn't been dry for two weeks. It was so quiet, the only sounds were those we made. And for all we knew, the closest life to us other than that in the water, was almost a thousand miles away. We were the only apparent sign of life in the entire world. There was no land for hundreds of miles, and the bottom of the ocean lay two miles under us. It was a day that made us feel as if we were in a big swimming pool and couldn't touch bottom.

Ever since we'd turned over we kept one of the inflatable rafts fastened to the bow. Charlie wanted to get some pictures of *Courageous*, so he went forward, untied the raft, and launched it. He got into the raft and I handed him the camera and an oar. We were "space men" with one of us tethered to our mother ship, *Courageous*. There were two occasions when we ventured out in the little rafts. Always tethered to *Courageous* with a fifteen-hundred-pound test line, we would take no chances of separating from *Courageous* to float away. And float away we would; we had already seen that anything accidentally dropped overboard floated away very quickly, like a small seat cushion that drifted off in a strong breeze. Even though we barely moved in the calm wind, the larger *Courageous* drifted away too quickly to retrieve anything dropped overboard. There was no way to turn *Courageous* around and sail up wind to retrieve something that fell overboard or blew out of the raft.

Not that there was much danger in Charlie's floating away with no breeze, but we kept the lines tied anyway. When he finished taking pictures, we secured the raft back on the bow. The solar still had made enough water so we had a good drink, and some excellent "after-dinner" conversation. Neither of us had had a bowel movement in two weeks, but since we weren't eating much, the condition was normal. We weren't constipated, we just didn't have anything in our intestines.

I became increasingly disappointed in not catching any fish. We hadn't even glimpsed any kind of fish since the shark. Not depicted on our charts, and not discovered until later, almost our entire expedition was in an area of the ocean called " the ocean desert," so named for the scarcity of marine life. By the time the Japanese Current flows south down the California and Mexican coasts, it has warmed considerably, and when it turns west with the trade winds, the water is relatively warm and continues to warm as it flows west. A defined quantity of warm water, as well as warm air, contains less oxygen than more dense cold water or air, and will not support the amount of marine life as will cold, oxygen-rich water. Plankton, the lowest of the ocean food chain, does not flourish in the warm, oxygen-poor environment, in turn drawing no small fish. If the small fish are not there, the larger predator fish go elsewhere to cooler, richer waters, and so on up the food chain

Destitute of fish, I was beginning to get a complex about fishing. When I tell fishermen that I trolled for fifty-six days, and twenty-seven hundred miles without catching a fish, I don't get invited on many fishing trips. I hope to prove to my fishermen friends that it wasn't my fault.

Henry, evidently discouraged with our lack of movement departed our company, and we never saw him again. I think Charlie felt somewhat defeated by Henry, even though he didn't put much effort again toward catching him.

We were becalmed three days. It was the most restful part of the entire trip, and the only time we fully relaxed. Three whole days of drying out! The boat was still and quiet; water didn't swish into our ears while we slept, nor was the boat burping that awful smell. There was no point in keeping a watch, so we didn't bother. Beyond those three halcyon days, the wind picked up to a normal, "Force 4", and once again we sailed westward.

I had read stories of castaways and sailors being "trapped" for weeks in the doldrums, and the thought crossed my mind that we could be here for a long time making little progress. We couldn't afford to be without wind for a long period as it would extend our trip far beyond 60 days. It began to appear that we were not going to catch any fish, so I was indeed concerned that we could not afford to float here too many days. Of course, there was nothing we could do about the fact that we had no wind. We just rested as much as we could, as we knew there were going to be days when we would have to borrow against all that saved energy.

The array of pictures we took of each other serves to document our changing physical appearances. The pictures show that we looked pretty good for people who hadn't eaten in a few weeks. The white stuff on our noses is zinc oxide. We kept it there so our noses wouldn't sunburn. The days became warmer, and we shed our wool shirts from time to time. In the warmer daytime air we now had to be careful to prevent our bodies from becoming so warm that we perspired and lost body fluids.

Besides the bout with cuts on our legs, we felt good the entire trip. Since we weren't exposed to other peoples' germs, the chance of contacting a communicable disease was pretty slim. We were enormously hungry, but no physical pain resulted. I cannot recall even having a headache on the trip. When we checked our vital signs on occasion, they merely indicated that our bodies were slowing down.

For instance, my resting pulse rate, normally about 60 beats a minute, dropped to 35 beats a minute showing how the body cooperates in conserving stored energy. Our body temperatures were almost always below normal by a couple of degrees, and the only times we felt noticeably weak were occasions when we were forced to move around a great deal.

The few movements taken to switch places for the watch change became a monumental effort. Sometimes we just stayed in the same position, not bothering to move when the other person took the watch. With the wind becoming steadier, we found we could sail for days, and never have to touch the helm. We just changed the position of the sail, and it adjusted our heading.

At night, if the wind were steady, we both would climb under the tarp and sleep. One night about two o'clock in the morning we were both sleeping soundly when all of a sudden there was something in the boat with us. Something very large lay across our bodies! We bolted up simultaneously, and yanked the tarp off. By the time we pushed the tarp off, whatever it was had jumped out of the boat and was gone. We never saw what it was, but the boat reeked with a fishy odor. We'd been slimed! If it wasn't Ghostbusters, whatever it was had jumped into the boat and left a coat of slime across the tarp. It happened so quickly that neither of us remembered hearing a splash as it dove back into the water. I estimated, by the part I felt on my body, that it must have weighed over sixty pounds.

After this mysterious episode, Charlie and I were so wired up that going back to sleep was impossible. Of course the first thing we thought about was food. Whatever was in the boat had been food, and we had missed it! Food had jumped right into the boat with us, and we hadn't even seen it. We sat there in a daze wishing the visitor would somehow have gotten caught in our sheet lines or something. Damn! We hated thinking that we missed what might have been our greatest, maybe only, opportunity for getting food. We were both hoping that whatever it was would jump back in. I'm sure that we probably scared it more than it scared us. If we'd had a little more composure, or had not been sleeping, we might have done things differently, like grabbing on to it. We were a little pissed at ourselves, but it all happened so quickly there wasn't time to do anything but scare the beejeeses out of the creature as it did us.

We got out the flashlight, checked the boat over for damage, and cleaned the slime off the tarp. I recalled a story about a fisherman turning on some night lights, and having flying fish jump into his boat. The lights evidently attracted the fish. Our fish episode gave me an idea. We had running lights that we didn't expect to use again, so I tied one of the lights up on a shroud line running to the mast. The light, I hoped, would attract fish to the boat. We'll never know what caused the first fish to jump into the boat, but I hoped to attract more with the light.

It wasn't until four or five o'clock in the morning that we crawled back to "bed". I slept later that morning than usual, as I was dead tired from the nighttime commotion. When I pulled the tarp off my head to look around the boat, lo and behold, there, lying right smack on the port pontoon, was a flying fish! The light must have attracted it just as I'd hoped. Unfortunately, it wasn't a very big flying fish about one inch long. In fact it was so little and dried out that we could not have divided it and had anything left to eat. So instead of eating it, we took a picture of it. We kept the light on at night for a few more nights, but never snared another fish with the light trap. The little flying fish dried on the boat and was finally washed off by a wave.

As the weather grew warmer and warmer we became even more ravenous. Whatever had jumped in the boat had been food, and we missed it! We just could not get over the fact that we may have missed the one lucky chance to obtain food. Food had jumped right into the boat with us, and we never had a chance to even see it.

One afternoon I was at the helm enjoying a beautiful day, when something in the water caught my eye. Something was bobbing up and down in the water about 20 yards ahead. I tired to change the heading so that I could come along side whatever it was that was floating in the water. It was a half-full whiskey bottle. I called Charlie to help me get the bottle, but we just could not change course enough to get over to the bottle. We watched as the bottle floated by not more than 10 feet away. It's not that I needed a drink so badly as it was that there were calories in that whiskey. Charlie made a joke that the bottle was probably one he had thrown off the carrier years before during a room inspection.

The Zodiac was holding up well. We thought we might have to keep inflating it from time to time during the trip, but that was not the case. Besides inflating it after the overturn we only had to get the foot pump out a couple of times to add more air to the chambers. It was truly a blessing that we did not have a bit of trouble with the Zodiac. I never expected it to remain inflated basically for the whole trip, but it did.

I still have *Courageous* thirty years later. She has suffered more from my moving her around for thirty years than she did on the trip. One can still see writing on the boat that had to do with our navigation. There is still a hole in the bottom where a fish bit into it, more of that later. As of this writing West Marine, a company that sell boating gear, has plans to display *Courageous* in one of its stores. I hope she is put on display because she took great care of us and deserves a place of honor.

Half a league, half a league,
Half a league onward.
—Alfred, Lord Tennyson

X

Halfway There

August 4th, was an important day for a couple of reasons. First, I finally recorded accurate sunrise and sunset times that absolutely pin-pointed our position. We were at one-thirty-five degrees west, and twenty-four degrees twenty minutes north. It was our one-month anniversary at sea, and we were just under half-way across the Pacific.

Up to this date I had applied compass variation improperly, and so began the process of backtracking my DR headings and distances. I found that my error had taken us no more than 40 miles from the new position that I calculated with the Solargram.

Charlie and I celebrated our anniversary by each having our one piece of candy, and an extra large drink of water at lunch time. We used the last of the water we gathered from the fog weeks earlier. We never again obtained any more water from Mother Nature, but as we moved west, the days became brighter, and the solar stills made enough water to keep us alive. We never, ever got enough water, but at least we were getting a drink every day now, at least 8 to 10 oz. each.

We were both considerably skinnier than when we left. When I showed Charlie my legs, normally rather large with large calves, they were nothing but skin and bone. I could barely raise a muscle in my legs, and could move the flesh of my calf around as if it were made of jello. Charlie too was left with very little muscle in his legs. He and I could fit our legs into some of the skinny new pants fashions, in fact we might even pass as two slim male models.

On this our one-month anniversary, we discovered that we were averaging forty-eight miles a day overall. Our best day's run had been almost seventy miles, and our worst was less than nine.

There was some very good sailing weather for the ensuing week, the winds blew a steady sixteen knots almost from due east. Thankful for the rest we had while we were becalmed, we knew we hadn't made much progress, and that again was discouraging.

Another cause for celebration was August 8th, when we crossed one-thirty-nine degrees west longitude marking the half way point of our trip. More appropriately, it would have been half-way had we sailed straight to Hawaii. It was good to be at the half-way point, because at last we could see we were closing in on Hawaii.

On the evening of August 10th, the wind began to increase. By two o'clock on the morning of the 11th, it blew a steady thirty knots. By four o'clock, as experience has proved, we could expect the seas to catch up with the winds, and we would be in for some work helming the boat. I untied the sheets from the helm to keep the boat on a heading with stern to the waves as we sailed. Just before sunrise the boat came down the side of a large wave, and the port side began to lift out of the water. Charlie and I both leapt to portside, and the pontoon came down. But that was enough to scare us once again into pulling down the sail and putting out the sea anchors. This time the seas weren't nearly so large as those we had before, but now we were considerably weaker. It was the absolute limit of our remaining energy to helm the boat in the big waves. Neither of us could stay at the helm for more than two hours in these sea conditions.

A feeling of total helplessness and exhaustion came over me in these miserable conditions. I was worn out, and I vented my anger at Mother Nature. When dawn broke and we studied the oncoming waves, we decided they didn't present such a great danger, and that we needed to keep sailing. It was tempting to just keep the sea anchors out, and lay in the boat to wait out the storm as that took little energy. Now slightly beyond our half-way mark, I began to worry about things other than survival. Charlie and I each had a two-month leave from the reserves, and needed to get to Hawaii before September 4th. We needed our jobs, and began to feel some pressure to continue sailing even in marginal conditions.

We took in the sea anchors and raised the sail. It was a grueling job to keep the boat on a heading in the waves. I cursed the waves as I worked to keep us on course. There was no way that we could continue to do this for many days, it was draining what remained of our, "reserve energy." For two days the wind blew, and the seas crashed into the boat. There were times when we could stay at the helm for only an hour before trading off, and aside from robbing us of energy, we were becoming very dehydrated. I didn't mind the starving, but dehydration was not only physically painful, it was mentally agonizing.

The ocean water was so blue, clear, and cold and I was so thirsty from the labor of helming, that I decided to take a drink of straight sea water. I dipped my bottle in the sea, and drank about ten ounces of sea water. To my surprise, it didn't taste salty at all. It tasted like spring water. I wasn't sure if I were going nuts or what. I was tempted to drink more, but scared that I just wasn't tasting the salt for some reason. Charlie and I talked about the possibility that some areas of the ocean might be less salty than others. I'd heard of undersea springs that flowed deep in the oceans. Maybe we were over a fresh spring that was feeding into the ocean from miles below us. We may have been one of the few sailors that were that close to the water for that many days, and maybe we had indeed discovered that some parts of the ocean were not salty at all. Nevertheless it was a great drink, and unlike the water from the solar stills, it was nice and cool. I did not get sick from drinking the water nor did I get diarrhea.

Because we had experienced the loss of taste insofar as the candy was concerned, I thought that perhaps we had become inured to a salt taste. Not wanting to take chances, I didn't drink any more straight sea water as a matter of habit, although no problems developed from what I had drunk. Later on, I tried some more sea water just to confirm the lack of a salt taste from the clear, blue water, but the taste from a different location was very salty. This convinced me further that I'd had a drink of sea water in an area of the ocean that wasn't as salty for some unexplained reason.

After three days the wind died down to the normal Force 4. We bailed water, and rested. We were worn out. On the afternoon of August 13th, we both lay on top of the tarp catching catnaps. I happened to look east into a beautiful, clear blue sky when something caught my eye. "Look", I yelled to Charlie as I pointed up to the east.

There, coming toward us was a big orange ball. I recognized it immediately as a Braniff Airline's Boeing 747. In those days Braniff Airline out of Dallas, Texas, painted their planes bright orange or turquoise, and I had heard or read that Braniff flights out of Dallas, Texas, used their bright orange Boeing 747 for the Hawaii run. We scrambled about the boat to get out the emergency radio to give him a condition report. We could see that he was going to pass directly over us which would give us a good fix on our position. It took awhile to open the boxes, and get out the radios. I marked the time the plane was directly overhead so we could backtrack his position to our location. He was almost out of sight by the time we made our first call.

"Braniff aircraft westbound at 145 degrees west, this is *Courageous* on 121.5. Over".

A few seconds later Braniff responded. He was probably in shock at someone calling him on emergency frequency.

"Aircraft calling on 121.5, this is Braniff 501, say again. Over." Braniff's cryptic reply in the parlance of air-to-air communication.

"Braniff 501 this is the raft *Courageous* calling, how do you hear? Over."

"*Courageous*, is that correct? This is Braniff 501. Read you loud and clear. Go ahead. Over."

"Braniff, affirmative, this is the raft *Courageous*. We are two souls sailing from San Francisco to Hawaii. You just passed over us about two minutes ago, if you're the orange 747 west bound. Over."

"That's us *Courageous*, do you need assistance? Over."

"Negative, we request that you take a phone number to make a collect call to my wife, Judi, and let her know you talked with us. Over."

"Be glad to *Courageous*. Ready to copy. Go ahead."

"The number is: area code 714-567-8989. Ask for Judi. She is normally home after five o'clock local time San Francisco. If you get an answering machine, please leave your number. She will return the call. Please report that we are okay and give her our position. Over."

"Copied *Courageous*. How long have you guys been down there? Over."

"We left San Francisco July 4th. Estimate Hawaii in about two weeks. Can you give us your present position? Over. "

"Roger, standby."

Braniff gave us his position, and after backtracking, I determined we were about 20 miles from where I thought we were.

"Braniff, if you have the time could you tell me who won Wimbeldon? Over."

"Just a minute, *Courageous*. Jimmy Conners won the men's and Chris Evert won the women's. Did you know that Nixon resigned? Over."

"Your kidding, who's President?"

"Gerald Ford is the new President. Over"

Charlie and I looked at each other with the same question on our minds, who is Gerald Ford?

I wanted to check the accuracy of my watch for navigational purposes, and this was a super time to do so.

"Braniff, can you give us a time hack? Over."

The Braniff pilot patched us in to "WWV", the universal coordinated time radio station, and we corrected our watches to the most precise time in the world. Once that was done, we couldn't resist asking him about our favorite topic.

"Braniff, thanks for the news, and the time hack. We got a good copy. One last thing, you guys want to drop us some food? Over."

"*Courageous*, we would love to do that, but we can't get the door open. We are having steak today. I guess you guys are eating lots of fish? Over."

Charlie and I visualized the first class section in Braniff. We'd be sitting in big, leather, dry chairs, sipping wine, and biting into juicy steaks, baked potato, and hot bread.

"Believe it or not Braniff, we haven't caught a fish yet. We're living on our own body fat and some candy. The fishing is bad to say the least, or maybe it's the fishermen. Thanks again for all the information. We appreciate your making the call. We have a limited amount of battery power so we'd better sign off. Maybe will catch you on the return trip. Thanks again for the information. *Courageous* out."

"Good luck, *Courageous*. Braniff 501 out."

Contact with the outside world once again brought our spirits up. We had just over 700 miles to Hawaii. With the trade winds blowing steadily, we'd be there in 12 days, or sooner if the winds held up. I couldn't stop thinking about the food being served on Braniff. I just knew there were people up there who wouldn't even want their meals, and how much I wanted what they didn't. We also thought about all those people being in Hawaii in less than two hours, enjoying warm beaches, or the comfort of soft, dry beds.

Two weeks didn't seem that long now. The next day we were still in good spirits from our conversation with Braniff. Charlie must have felt either really good or really dirty, because he wanted to launch one of the rafts and take a bath. I know I was filthy, but I didn't know whether or not I wanted to take a bath. I was getting used to being dirty. Besides, the water temperature was not more than 72 degrees, and felt colder.

Nevertheless, Charlie was determined, and it was a beautiful, warm day. He launched the raft, making sure the line was tied securely to *Courageous*. We were moving along at about 2 knots, if Charlie and the raft were to become separated in this wind it would be extremely difficult to get back to *Courageous*, even if I took down the sail. Charlie let the little raft drift to the stern while he stripped down. I told him if the line gave way not to worry about the raft, but grab the line or swim to *Courageous* as fast as possible. There would be absolutely no way to paddle the little raft fast enough to catch *Courageous* judging from the speed with which items had drifted out of sight when we had inadvertently dropped them overboard.

Charlie decided that he would dive into the water, and swim to the raft. I thought this a little risky and daring. There was no telling how much strength I had left in me, and I certainly didn't have enough fat on me to float as I normally would. Charlie stood at the stern while I got the camera. When everything was ready Charlie took the dive, and quickly swam to the raft. I could tell from his screams that the water was as cold as I thought. Charlie pulled himself into the raft and began bathing. He looked like he was having a ball. I began to think that maybe I would also take a bath also.

When Charlie had finished, I pulled Charlie back to *Courageous*, he climbed out, and I climbed into the raft. Once I got used to the cold water, the bath was great. Although it took a lot of energy, it felt good to be clean. I almost didn't want to put my stinking clothes back on. We took pictures of each other as we stood holding on to the mast and shroud lines. We were surely getting very skinny. I estimated Charlie to be down to 135 to 140 pounds. When I stood up to have my picture taken, I discovered how weak my legs had become. I could barely hold myself up. My legs had no power whatsoever. I shook as I stood there, hoping my legs wouldn't collapse under me. After we secured the little raft and clothed ourselves, we had to rest. We felt great, but were tired. I was glad that we had taken the bath because I knew I wouldn't have the strength to do it again.

As intended, we were to take our vital signs on a regular basis, but as we got weaker it got to be too much trouble to do the tests. For instance, the medical equipment was not designed to be used in such harsh environment, it was difficult to hear a heartbeat through the stethoscope with wind blowing through the ear pieces. But August 18th, dawned bright and clear, the seas were running the normal 3 to 4 feet with a very gentle swell, and we decided it was a good day to take our vital signs including blood pressure.

We got out the equipment, and Charlie was going to play doctor first. He wrapped the blood pressure cuff around my upper arm, and pumped it up. He then placed the end of the stethoscope on the inside of my elbow, and began to release the air. Slowly the cuff relaxed on my arm as Charlie stared at the gauge. When he finished, he tapped on the gauge the way we tapped the gauges in our navy aircraft. If they "fluttered" a bit, we knew they were functioning and not "dead." I asked him if something were wrong. Charlie said he didn't know, but he'd take my pressure again.

Once again he pumped up the cuff and it squeezed my arm. We did this three times, and it was beginning to hurt my arm.

"What the hell are you doing?" I asked.

"Well, either the instruments are failing or you are,"

Charlie kidded.

At least I hoped he was kidding. He told me that he could not get a diastolic pressure, and that the systolic pressure was no more than 60. My normal blood pressure is 120 over 80, but now it was reading 60 over zero. I took Charlie's pressure, and got almost the same reading. This convinced me that our pressure had indeed dropped that much for a couple of reasons. First, when I had tried to stand up a few days earlier after I took my bath, I had become somewhat dizzy. Our current low blood pressure would account for that dizziness. Secondly, pressure instruments are very simple, consisting of few simple parts that are not prone to failure. In addition, we had not used the instruments that much, and had kept them in a watertight box the entire trip.

It worried me that our pressure had dropped so drastically. Our urine had become so dark and thick, I knew we needed that diastolic pressure to keep fluids flowing through our kidneys. The doctors had briefed us on what could happen to us physically, but there had been no mention of the drop in blood pressure, except that we might expect kidney problems from the lack of drinking water. It wasn't clear at this point if the doctors' caution referred to the lack of liquids, or that our blood pressure was going to drop as our bodies consumed themselves.

Although our urine was dark, and we had not had a bowel movement in over a month, we felt fine. There was no pain at all in the kidney area. We continued to urinate just about the same quantity of liquid that we took in. We weren't at all worried about the lack of a bowel movement because we were not taking in enough food to create a stool. My major concern about the entire crossing had been that one of us would become sick, but there we were, both doing fine. We were both alert, in fact we devised a little game remembering the names of every teacher we'd had from the first grade all the way through college. I invite anyone who has been out of school for ten years to try that mental exercise! I had never remembered all my teachers' names before; perhaps the quietness of the raft and the absence of distractions enabled me to think more clearly than ever before. I think there might be a case to be made about the improvement in mental skills as the body uses up fat. Maybe my body was cleansed of impurities, and my brain benefited from the blood that would have normally gone to my stomach for digestion, and on to other organs. We both felt extremely alert and mentally fit.

A Coast Guard helicopter with Dr. Lee in the basket. Dr. Lee flew out to the cutter to see if we were strong enough to be moved to Tripler Army Hospital.

Charlie and George being interviewed by a TV station out of Honolulu. We had done it! We proved the survival kit worked.

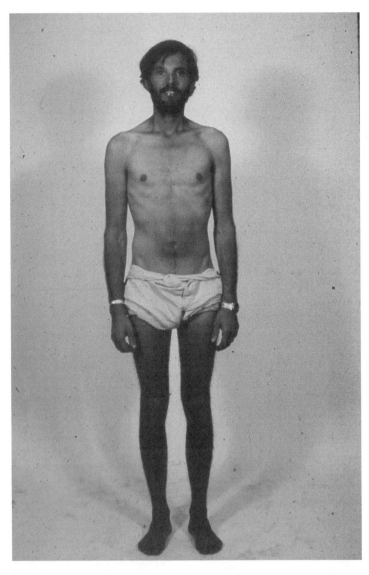

George, as he looked the day after he was picked up. It may not look like it, but I felt great!

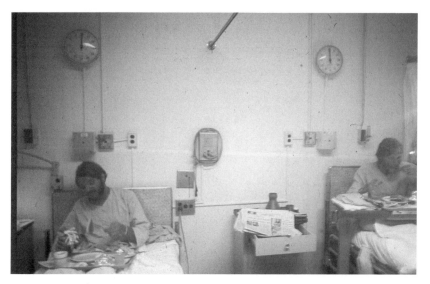

Charlie and George enjoying their first breakfast of pancakes at Tripler Army Hospital. That's all Charlie could talk about during the trip, pancakes.

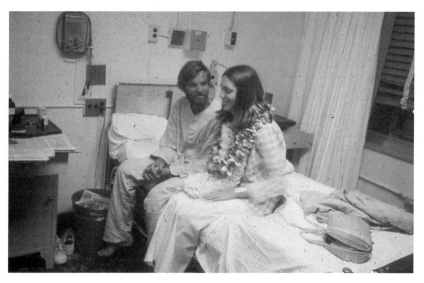

Judi flew to Hawaii to meet George at the hospital. She was a little surprised to see George as he now had a beard and had lost 56lb. George still tells people he had to do what Judi told him to because she outweighed him. She told me not to mention that in a book so I agreed.

Launching Courageous 30 miles from San Francisco. Our friends looking down from the large yacht that took us to sea. It was a little strange watching that yacht motor back towards the Golden Gate as we headed to Hawaii.

George coming aboard Courageous after having been in the one person raft taking a bath. It took so much energy we never did this again.

Charlie standing holding on to the mast with the flag in the background.

Side view of George. His weight had dropped from 184lb. to about 135lb in 49 days. Surprisingly there was absolutely no physical discomfort in starving.

George washing his underwear. We wore wool clothing because it retained its insulation value even when wet. We poured salt water over our clothes to keep from loosing water to perspiration, but occasionally we had to rinse our clothing as the salt buildup made them very stiff after awhile.

Charlie enjoying his bath. The tether holding the two rafts together can be seen in the water. We quickly realized that anything dropped in the water drifted away very quickly so the nylon line was indeed our safety line.

We knew the merry world was round,
And we might sail for evermore.
-Alfred, Lord Tennyson

XI

Closing in on Hawaii

It was August 22nd, and we had not seen a ship for over a month and a half. Sometimes I thought I heard noises at night as my ear pressed against the bottom of the raft, but there were no ships to be seen. I wondered sometimes if I were hearing submarines operating beneath us. That may sound like a far-fetched idea, but I believe that on one occasion, a disaster at sea involved a sailboat and a submarine. Because the sailboat sank, and the incident happened at night, there was never proof that a submarine had actually been involved in the sinking. Accounts of the survivors lead me to believe that only a collision with a submarine could have caused the damages incurred by the boat. Even though whale-ramming has caused some sailboat sinkings, the violent nature of structural damage to the high freeboard of this particular incident appears to rule out a whale.

On this day I was at the helm enjoying the bright day, the steady wind, and the relatively calm seas. I had my back to the stern, and my right elbow on top of the stern board. Charlie was portside, sitting sidewise, and looking out to starboard. All of a sudden Charlie jerked toward me looking aft into the water.

"You better check your six," he advised. This was aviation

fighter pilot lingo meaning: "look to the rear for danger." I twisted my neck to look behind me. First I noticed a very large fin about a foot out of the water. I slowly moved my elbow back into the raft.

Charlie moved toward the stern as I came to my knees to turn toward the stern also. The shark's head had been no more than a foot and a half from my elbow, right between the two stern tubes. Its head was so large that it almost filled the entire area between the two tubes. The shark cruised around us very slowly. Its tail movement was almost imperceptible as it swept slowly back and forth. What alarmed me was that the shark had come so close to my arm without making a sound. I should have been scared, but it wasn't the shark itself that scared me.

My photos show there is something white floating on a line in the water behind the raft near the shark. It was my sneaker. As I had grown up in West Texas, I did a lot of fishing for catfish. Anyone who has ever fished for catfish knows that the bait must exude a very foul odor in order to attract them. In fact, it has to stink rotten! I remembered this as I wasn't having much luck with worms and lures, and figured I needed to change my bait. The worst stink in the raft was my tennis shoes, so I took one of my shoes which was stored away, cut it in half, and attached the two halves to large hooks on a 125-pound test steel line. Then I threw them overboard leaving the lines attached to cleats on the stern of the raft.

I hadn't caught any fish so far with my lure, but I believe the shark was attracted to the smell of the tennis shoes. We watched the shark, later identified for us as a "Great White."

The movie "Jaws" had not yet been produced, but "Jaws" notwithstanding, neither Charlie nor I had developed a built-in fear of shark. It swam around the stern of the raft, then backed off about twenty feet. Then it moved around to starboard, and once again began to approach the raft. I saw its mouth open as it came closer to the tennis shoe trailing to starboard. It was going to take the shoe, and I didn't want the line attached to our raft. This was certainly not a fish we wanted to catch. And we certainly did not want a fish that was bigger than the raft, trashing around on a steel line attached to the raft. I jumped to the stern to untie the line, and was able to free the line just before the shark snapped its jaws, taking the shoe and the line with it. The shark then swam around with the steel line hanging out of its mouth. It was sure to take the other shoe on the port side. I began to untie that shoe before he made his next approach. Never expecting such a big fish, much less a Great White, I had wrapped the line around the cleat a number of times. When Charlie called to me that the shark was making his approach toward the other shoe, I hurried as quickly as I could, but felt the line yanked hard from my hands. I shook my hands free of the coiled line just as I felt the tremendous power of that animal pull the line from my hands. A split second later the line would have snapped around my wrist, and either the shark would have pulled me into the water or the line would have severed my hand. Almost becoming a version of Captain Ahab's tangle in the fouled harpoon line, I was one lucky fisherman that I didn't tangle in that line.

Undoubtedly, had the shark taken the line fastened to the raft, we might have had a wild ride, and/or sustained major damage. When he came up along the portside, his size astounded us. He was easily the size of *Courageous* at 15 feet 5 inches! It was the largest fish I had ever seen, and truly magnificent. It never swam more than two feet below the surface so we could see it clearly as it swam around us.

After a couple of turns around the raft, the shark swam off about 40 feet to port side. His whole upper body broke the surface, with its dorsal fin out of the water by a foot or more. Suddenly it's tail whipped violently, and it struck out toward us at a high rate of speed. A wake of white water formed around its fin as it cut through the water. I yelled to Charlie that he was about to ram us! We each grabbed a side of the raft and held on. The aerodynamic body looked like a torpedo aimed for us. Just before it got to the raft it sounded, and went right under us. We felt the water compress under us. We looked to starboard expecting to see it exit on the other side of the raft, but we only saw a shadow moving deep and away. We wanted to believe that it lunged after the small fish that swam under the raft. We never saw the shark again. From that time forward, I made it a habit to look aft now and again just to check my six. The episode with the Great White convinced me that I was not going to jump into the water for a swim.

On the morning of August 22nd, I wakened before sunrise and got a good fix on sunrise for navigation. It was a clear morning, and the sun began to light the eastern sky as dawn approached. Waiting for the sun, I looked around and saw something on the western horizon. It was still dark toward the west, but there was definitely an object on the horizon. I watched for awhile, and it grew larger. A ship? I shook Charlie awake to tell him about the ship which I thought might pass close by. Charlie crawled out from under the tarp, and we sat watching the object grow larger and closer. We decided to light some flares, and hoped someone on the ship would see us. As it drew nearer, we saw that it was an aircraft carrier, and that it was going to pass very close to us. We unpacked our military survival radio which carries the military UHF guard frequency, 243.0 mHz. Since it was a carrier, we assumed they would be monitoring the guard emergency frequency even though they were not conducting flight operations.

The carrier was closing in fast. We couldn't tell if it was going to just pass by or run over us. I had first thought that we would experiment with the flares just to see if the carrier saw us. Then as it appeared to be coming right at us, I thought we had better get its attention because there was no way we could move fast enough to avoid being run over. I lit a couple of flares, and Charlie broadcast a few calls on the radio. There was no response. As the carrier drew closer we could see there was no one on deck. We joked that everyone was probably below drinking coffee. The carrier passed no more than a quarter to a half-mile away. We continued to call on the radio, and I set off a couple more smoke flares. Still no response from the carrier. As a couple of carrier pilots ourselves, we knew there had to be at least 1500 men aboard, but there was no activity on deck, nor anyone monitoring the radios. I, at that instant, developed a strong sympathy for the castaway who might have sent up those flares, called on his radio, waved his shirt; or whatever, only to watch that huge ship sweep past and disappear over the horizon. It was truly amazing that no one saw us, or saw our flares. As the ship slid past we thought of all the food and water she had aboard. God, it would have been great just to have had her stop and talk to us. We could have been run over by that ship and no one would ever have known.

The winds began to shift from the east to the southeast, my newest concern. It was becoming noticeably more difficult to maintain a westerly heading, and we were drifting north. Because of my earlier navigational error, we were always further north than intended, but now it was becoming impossible to correct to the south. For days the wind had continued to blow us northwest. We were still on a line north of Maui, and it was beginning to look impossible that we could sail down to Maui. I hoped the wind would shift back coming from the east, because it was beginning to look serious. Unknown to us a somewhat unusual weather pattern had caused the winds to shift blowing from the south, "Kona" winds, named for a town located on the Big Island which was the southern most island.

On the 23rd of August we were 170 miles northeast of Maui, and the winds continued to blow us northwest. That wouldn't have been so bad except the Islands run from southeast to northwest. Although we were sailing northwest, the islands were falling away faster than we could sail west to them. The further north we sailed, the further away the islands became.

By August 26th, we had traveled 120 miles to the northwest, and were still 125 miles from Oahu even though we had covered more than 70 miles to the west. If we continued northwest, in two days we would find ourselves 60 miles further west, but 180 miles away from the nearest island, Kauai. Well, if we missed Hawaii, I told Charlie that Japan was our next best bet for land. It was a slim joke, but the situation was indeed worrisome.

Finally, on the evening of the 26th of August, the wind began to shift coming from the east. We set the sail as far to the south as possible until it began luffing. I checked our heading, and plotted the point where this course would take us. If the wind remained steady, we would make landfall somewhere on Oahu or Kauai. We suspected that we must be getting close to the islands, because we could see and hear aircraft arriving and departing.

For the first time we began to see fish in the water. Maui Maui, the dolphin fish, or dorado as it is called, from time to time darted past the raft. They were a beautiful fish with glowing blue and yellow colors. The dorado swam at times right under the raft, and often within what looked like an easy reach. I couldn't see how I could help but catch some of them with my hook and line. I put out a spinner, but didn't get a bite. We were moving very slowly, probably less than three knots, and the dorado were not the least bit interested in the bait. I left the lines out day and night just in case we got lucky.

We were finally making better progress to the west as the wind shifted somewhat. A fearsome thought crossed my mind a number of times that we might sail right between Oahu and Kauai, and not make landfall. How ironic that we could sail almost 3000 miles yet not make landfall on islands that were about 60 miles apart. It began to appear that we might do exactly that, sail right between the two. There remained only one logical course of action in our choice of sailing strategies. We had to sail as far south as possible as if we intended to make Oahu. Then if we were unable to make Oahu, we were left to sail north to Kauai. If we tried to sail directly to Kauai, however, and inadvertently drifted north, there were no islands north to serve as a "safety net" except Midway, another 900 miles to the northwest.

The prospect of missing Hawaii became real enough to take very seriously. We both felt very good albeit weak, and low on energy. It was obvious that we had lost a good deal of body weight, and we could expect to lose more weight if we missed the Hawaiian Islands. It would take another two weeks to reach Midway. And Midway, unlike the Hawaiian Islands, is nothing but an atoll, a small island a few feet above sea level at its highest point. We would have to sail directly to Midway, and very close in order just to be able to see it. If we were to live another two weeks or more, we would need additional food. The solar stills were making more water than at any other time during the trip so we felt safe with our water supply, but the 60-day limit was nearing.

Because we were in waters where shipping traffic might be present, we began to keep our nightly watches again. We also thought we might be able to see lights on the islands at night. We talked until late on the night of August 26th. Discussing our options, we decided to head for Oahu and see where we might be the next evening. We both hoped to see lights that night, but we were still much too far away.

Charlie took the watch from midnight to four on the morning of August 27th, as I pulled the tarp over me, and went to sleep. About 3:30 that morning I woke up or something wakened me. I wasn't sure what it was, but I knew something wasn't right. Something was different. Stories of sailors, especially about those who sailed boats across an ocean by themselves, tell of men becoming so attuned to the action and noises of their boats that the smallest change wakes them instantly from even a sound sleep. I had that feeling.

I pulled the tarp off, and looked aft. There was Charlie, leaning over the stern as if he might be throwing up. My worst fear was that one of us would become sick and need medical help. I yelled, "Charlie, are you OK?"

Charlie spun around, and held up a sopping wet, brown bird in his hands. I couldn't believe my eyes! "How did you catch him?" I asked.

"I sat here half asleep when I heard wings flapping. It landed on the starboard solar still, and I just sat there and watched it, not moving a muscle. After a short while the bird folded its wings, and sort of squatted on its legs. I sat up very slowly, and began to run my hands up the sides of the solar still, then I lunged for it, and got hold of it. When I had it in my hands, it began to bite my fingers. The only thing I could think of was to drown the damn thing, so I held it under water until it stopped biting."

"Damn," I said in amazement. Captain Rickenbacker wrote that he had success in catching a sea bird by hand during World War II, but that was about the only account I could remember of a castaway catching a sea bird by hand. I was amazed. After almost two months, we had caught our first food by hand! It was laughable, and we did laugh about it. I told Charlie that from my upbringing in Texas, and having a dad who raised chickens, the way you "do in" a bird is to wring its neck, as I circled my hands in a twisting motion in demonstration.

The bird smelled like shit, and I mean shit literally. Even though we hadn't eaten for days, I was not hungry enough to eat that bird raw. I asked Charlie to just put it up forward and wait until daylight. Maybe then we could cut some meat off the breast. When it was my turn for the watch, Charlie went forward and put the dead bird on the bow, and I sat down in the stern to take the helm. Charlie pulled the tarp over himself and sacked out. I couldn't get the thought of Charlie catching that bird out of my mind. Gosh, Charlie was right up there with Rickenbacker as an American Hero!

Sitting there thinking, I heard a flapping noise just over the right side of my head. When I turned my head slightly, there was a bird sitting right on top of the same solar still where Charlie's bird had landed. Not more than a foot-and-a-half away was my chance for glory. I almost stopped breathing in trying to be still. I watched the bird for about a minute as it settled itself on the still, and I let it sit there a little while hoping it was asleep. Slowly I turned and began to move my hands up the side of the still. I had some real doubts that I could catch a bird by hand, but I was going to give it my best try.

The bird never moved as I got my hands right up to its side. When I thought I was close enough, I made a quick grab. I got it! Or more properly, it got me. I found out what Charlie was talking about. The darn bird began to peck at my fingers, and it threw me off guard, first for being such a small bird, and second for having such power in its jaws. True to what I told Charlie about Texas, I grabbed the bird by the head, and swung it around like a helicopter. Blood, guts, and feathers began to fly everywhere. The commotion woke up Charlie, and there I was with the bird in one hand, and a big smile on my face. I was so proud. I was right up there with Rickenbacker, and I hadn't been outdone by Charlie. I got my bird.

Unfortunately my bird didn't smell any better than Charlie's. I put it up forward on the bow alongside Charlie's. Again we agreed it would be better to wait until daylight to eat our catches. There was still some time before daybreak, so we went back to our positions, Charlie to sleep, and I, to watch. My mind was fairly made up right there, that even though I hadn't eaten anything substantial for a long period, I was never going to be hungry enough to eat those raw birds. We were both doing well physically, but my stomach would not have held down raw bird.

It did occur to me, however, that the bird might make excellent fish bait. There were dorado in the area and with some fresh cut meat as bait they might either take a baited hook, or swim close enough to the raft to spear. The breast of the bird could be edible, and I thought I'd give it a try, but the remainder of the bird could be used as bait.

As the sun rose, I could again see flashes of fish swimming past the raft. I woke Charlie up, and pointed out to him the fish all around us. He crawled forward to get the birds, but found only one. My bird was gone, nowhere to be seen, and the mystery was never solved. I told Charlie that I put the bird's neck in so many knots that it probably helicoptered off the raft.

I got out the knife and cut through the bird's skin in the

breast area. It was surprising how small the bird actually was. It had looked a lot bigger at night, there just wasn't much there. I finally succeeded in getting some of the breast meat cut away, but the whole thing smelled so badly that I didn't even want to taste the meat. Charlie inspected the bloody mess, and he had second thoughts on eating the bird for fear of getting sick. We decided to use the bird as bait.

Because of our alarming encounter with the shark, we had some reservations about putting the bloody bait in the water. We decided it was worth the risk, and if we saw a shark we'd cut bait. The dorado were still with us swimming past the raft as if they knew we had a meal for them. Charlie got out the spear, and made sure everything was ready to shoot. I finished cutting the bird into small pieces, and we put the bait into the water on either side of the raft. Charlie was on his knees leaning over the side with spear in hand ready to fire.

Since Charlie had more experience with a spear than I, he got to be the shooter. The dorado began to swim closer to the raft, and came up nearer the surface. They swam past quickly, but not nearly so fast as the previous day. Then Charlie saw a fish that looked as if it were going to swim right along side the raft. I could see Charlie was going to take a shot at this fish as his legs and arms tensed. He watched the fish as it came closer, and then in a flash the spear went flying through the water. Nothing! Charlie pulled the spear back to the raft, and pulled the surgical tubing back to the cocked position.

When I was in college I used to hunt fish using bow and arrows. I learned how to compensate when viewing an object in water, that because of a physics phenomena called, "refraction" objects appear closer to the surface of the water than they really are. Charlie had a lot more experience with spears than I, but when you're in the water with the fish, as was his experience, there is no refraction. I suggested that he might try to shoot a little below where he thought the fish actually was.

The first shot must have scared them; it took them a few minutes to come around to the raft again. We seemed to be in a school of five to six fish. We saw that they were actually circling the raft making passes at the bait. Once again Charlie grew tense as a fish made an approach. Again the spear went flying, and at almost the same instant the water began to churn when the spear made contact, and we had our first edible fish.

Before we got the fish into the raft, we witnessed one of the strangest things I have ever seen. Charlie pulled the fish, which weighed about 15 pounds, toward the raft, and all the other dorado came up to the speared fish and circled him. Their bodies stood almost vertical in the water with their heads almost at the surface. They were not trying to eat the speared fish, they simply looked like they were there trying to help. They stayed almost motionless. If I had had a large net, I could have caught all the other dorado easily as they positioned themselves around the dying fish.

We pulled the fish into the raft, and it tried valiantly to escape the inevitable as I pounced on top of it. I hit it over the head with the knife and quieted it. Better to knock it out rather than let it flail around, and cause me to cut into an inflation chamber by trying to stab it. The fish finally gave up, and I sliced off its head.

The raft was full of blood, and we had to take precaution that no blood get into the water around us. We were the hunters, and didn't want to become the hunted. I knew we were going to eat this fish. And it didn't smell badly, at least compared to the bird. I began to cut large, beautiful chunks of pink flesh from its body.

The other dorado didn't leave the area, but continued to swim around the raft. They swam much deeper however, and almost seemed to know how far the spear would reach. As I was busy cutting the flesh, Charlie cleaned the raft of blood and guts. We could not throw the "bloody mess" overboard lest we attract another shark. But, since we had the sail up, we decided to sail away from the bloody scene, and throw the mess overboard as far down wind as possible.

I finished cleaning the fish, and things settled down a bit. We decided to give the raw fish a try. We each ate less than three ounces, not because it tasted bad, but because we weren't sure how our bodies would react. The flesh was moist and had a pleasant taste so far as raw fish goes. Neither of us was keen on raw fish, but this wasn't too bad. Although we had ample water to drink, there was always the concern of eating too much protein to cause dehydration. As I mentioned before, protein takes more water for digestion and elimination than any other type food.

We decided to hang the remainder of the fish over the shroud lines to let it sun dry. Of course we didn't plan to continue the expedition past Hawaii, but there was that nagging chance that we could miss the islands, in which case we'd need the fish. We emptied one of the water bottles, deciding to use it for packing the dried fish. At this point we felt pretty good about ourselves, and I had to admit Charlie had done a great job in hitting that fish. I was proud that I had done enough research to recognize a spear as a valuable asset.

A couple of hours had passed since we killed the fish, and we settled down into our normal, sedentary routine. When we felt we had distanced ourselves enough from the original scene of the spearing, we threw the blood and remaining fish parts overboard. The dorado were still with us, but we had enough fish to last a long time. It would have been nice to have another fish, but they were not coming close enough for another shot.

I'll never forget what happened next. From out of nowhere there came a violent jolt from under the raft. Something had hit us with a solid thump that actually vibrated the entire raft. We sat bolt upright. Whatever had struck the raft demanded our full attention. We instinctively knew that we'd been hit with enough force to cause damage. Again the raft was struck from underneath! We jumped to the sides, and peered overboard into the crystal blue water. I saw fish flashing through the water at high speeds. It was the dorado! Four of them were attacking the raft. And believe me, a veritable attack it was.

In naval flight training we had a course in gunnery in which a tow plane pulls a target banner through the sky as we practiced shooting at it. The shooters would fly a pattern around the tow plane in a kind of circle where we would get above the target, then dive down for our shot. Well, these fish were doing exactly the same thing. They dove deep under the raft then came up almost vertically to hit the bottom of the raft. As soon as they hit the raft they swam away in a diving circle to attack again and again.

Charlie grabbed the spear, and began shooting at the fish as they came toward the raft.

"We're taking on water!" I shouted when I looked down to see that we had about two inches of water in the bottom of the raft. I wasn't worried about holes in the bottom of the raft, but I was extremely worried about one of the fish biting a hole in one or all of the inflation chambers. The latter would be a life threatening situation whereas the water in the bottom of the raft was simply an inconvenience.

Charlie hit one fish after another until we had killed all five of the fish. We must have had 50 pounds of fish after our fight. It was a bloody mess, and blood was seeping through the hole or holes in the bottom of the raft and into the water. I was sure that now we would attract shark. I cleaned the fish, and draped steaks for drying all over the raft.

It was a shame to have killed so many of those beautiful fish. We had more fish than we could possibly eat. However, if we missed the islands, we had enough to keep us alive for a long period. We cleaned the raft as well as we could, and threw the remains of the fish overboard.

We were fortunate that the fish did not bite through an air chamber, and that the water in the raft never got more than a couple of inches deep. I crawled forward to try to locate the source of the leak, and found a round hole about an inch across where a fish had bitten through. This was a defining point in the futility of patching kits for life rafts. There was no way to repair this kind of damage in mid ocean. The directions on the repair kit, very much like repair kits in all life rafts, instructed the occupant to dry the area prior to applying the patch. How ridiculous! The kit was obviously made by someone who had never been in a damaged life raft. Common sense makes it obvious that the area of a tube with a hole in it will sink lower than the tubes with no holes. If the area sinks below the water line, it would be impossible to dry the area prior to application of the patch. In the present case, we could have used a raft repair clamp, but we hadn't yet incorporated them into the survival kit.

We just had to sleep in water. We were used to water in the raft anyway, but it made it a little cold at night.

We surely enjoyed the raw fish. It didn't taste bad, and we held it down with no problem. It was actually better raw than dried out. It had been another day that we felt good about; we had each caught a bird, and had enough fish for at least two more months, and could see aircraft making approaches to Hawaii, even the wind was cooperating.

A WARM GREETING FOR AIRMEN WHO SET RECORD IN A NAVY JET
Mike Grant and his wife exchange kisses; Judy Sigler embraces her husband George

Longest nonstop Navy jet flight

By Don Martinez

The sleek KA-3B "Skywarrier" jet bomber gently touched down on the hot asphalt runway of the Alameda Navel Air Station, popped its drag chute and rolled to a stop in an uneventful landing.

But it wasn't so routine for the three Navy Reserve airmen who scrambled out of the aircraft late yesterday afternoon. They had just flown the plane non-stop from Rota, Spain, to the East Bay

facility in a 6,100-mile, 13-hour, record-breaking flight.

It was the largest non-stop flight of a Navy carrier- based tactical jet aircraft.

"It was touch and go a couple of times when we were refueling," explained Lt. George Sigler, the pilot. Rough mid-Atlantic weather "made things kind of busy," during the first two of four airrefuel-

ings Sigler said, "but once we were over the United States things calmed down a bit and the plane almost flew itself."

The other two crewmen were Lt. Mike Grant of San Leandro, Airman navigator, and Fred Carrigan of Alameda.

Grant said the plane averaged 464 miles per hour and flew at about 40,000 feet during most of the marathon flight.

George set the record for the longest flight of a single-piloted navy carrier based jet. After sending his message from Rota, Spain he knew the Navy either had to kick him out or make him a hero. They made him a hero.

RELEASED BY		DRAFTED BY		PHONE EXT NR	PAGE	PAGES
CAPT M. A. BENERO		LT. G. B. SIGLER			1	
DATE	TOR/TOD		ROUTED BY	CHECKED BY		OF 2
20 JULY 75						

MESSAGE NR	DATE/TIME GROUP		PRECE-DENCE	FLASH	IMMEDIATE	PRIORITY	ROUTINE
4540	291604Z		ACTION			XXXXXXX	
			INFO				

FM: COMNAVACT ROTA SP

TO: VAQ 208 NAS ALAMEDA

BT

UNCLAS // N05000 //

PROJECT AGILE DANCER/HOMEWARD BOUND

1. REQUEST COMNAVAIRRES ENDORSEMENT AND PAO SUPPORT WITH PROJECT "AGILE DANCER/HOMEWARD BOUND," WHICH WILL CONSIST OF THE LONGEST FLIGHT OF A CARRIER BASED TACTICAL JET AIRCRAFT DEPARTING ROTA 0900Z 31 JUL 75 AND LANDING NAS ALAMEDA, CA NON STOP. IN SUPPORT OF MARINE TRANSLANT "AGILE DANCER" A KA-3B AIRCRAFT FROM RESERVE SQUADRON VAQ 208 BASED AT NAS ALAMEDA WILL DEMONSTRATE THE LONG RANGE STRIKING CAPABILITIES OF A CARRIER BASED AIRCRAFT UTILIZING THE ASSESTS OF THE U. S. NAVY. THE KA-3B AIRCRAFT WILL BE FLOWN AND NAVIGATED BY TWO SELECTED AIR RESERVE OFFICER FROM VAQ 208 NAS ALAMEDA.

2. AFTER DEPARTING ROTA, SPAIN AND PERFORMING ROUTINE PATH FINDING DUTIES IN SUPPORT OF MARINE SQUADRON VMA 332 AND UPON RELEASE FROM PROJECT "AGILE DANCER" OVER GANDER NEWFOUNDLAND THE KA-3B WILL PROCEED DIRECTLY TO NAS ALAMEDA, CA ON PROJECT HOMEWARD BOUND.

A copy of the original message Sigler composed and had the Chief in Rota send to all the press agencies once he was airborne. It was really pure "BS". It is in this book because my navy friends always wondered how I got away with it.

NAVAL MESSAGE

RELEASED BY		DRAFTED BY		PHONE EXT NR		PAGE	PAGES
CAPT M. A. BUNERO		LT G. B. SIGLER				2	2
DATE 29 JULY 75	TOR/TOD		ROUTED BY	CHECKED BY		of	

MESSAGE NR	DATE/TIME GROUP	PRECE-DENCE	FLASH	IMMEDIATE	PRIORITY	ROUTINE
4540	291604Z	ACTION			XXXXXXX	
		INFO				

3. THIS FLIGHT WILL DEMONSTRATE THE READINESS OF THE NAVAL RESERVE
AND ITS CAPABILITIES OF SUPPORTING THE REGULAR NAVY AS THE AIRCRAFT AN
AND CREW ARE ALL ASSETS OF THE U. S. NAVAL AIR RESERVE.

4. THIS FLIGHT WILL BE THE "ICING ON THE CAKE" FOR A TWO WEEKS ACTIVE
DUTY PERIOD WHICH HAS SEEN THIS SQUADRONS AIRCRAFT IN SUPPORT OF THE
U. S. NAVY WITH CARRIER ON BOARD DELIVERY SERVICE ABOARD THE USS JFK
AND USS FORRESTAL, VIP SERVICE FROM A CARRIER TASK FORCE TO LAND
BASED FACILITIES, LOGISTICS SUPPORT WHICH WAS PARAMONT IN THE SUCCESS
OF PROJECT AGILE DANCER, AND AERIAL REFUELING DUTIES ALL OF WHICH
WERE PERFORMED WHILE OPERATING IN A FOREIGN ENVIRONMENT.

5. THE KA-3B AIRCRAFT WILL CARRY A COMMEMORATIVE FROM THE CO OF NAVSTA
ROTA, SP. TO THE CO OF NAS ALAMEDA. LT G. R. SIGLER SENDS.

BT

The Honolulu Advertiser's headlines after our arrival in Honolulu.

*To travel hopefully is a better thing than to arrive,
and the true successor is to labor.*
  —*Robert Louis Stevenson*

XII

Arrival in Hawaii

We hadn't made radio contact in a long time so I decided to make a call to report our arrival in Hawaiian waters, and that we might make landfall in less than a week. It was about 10:00 AM when I got on the radio. After a couple of calls in the "blind," a Japan Airline pilot answered. I told him who we were, and he seemed to know about our trip. While I talked with JAL, a Coast Guard C-130 broke into our conversation to request that I switch to UHF guard, 243.0 mHz. I signed off with the JAL captain, and switched to the military radio frequency where we could talk without cluttering the airwaves.

In no time I made contact with the C-130. The pilot said that he was in fact out looking for us. This surprised us because we had an agreement that they would allow us sixty days before alerting search agencies. This was only our 55th day! He went on to say that he had a message-in-hand designating our arrival as an official Navy project, and that the Navy had flown doctors to Hawaii in order to complete their research.

Charlie could hear the conversation, and we looked at each other in stunned surprise. Surprising us most was the term, "official Navy project." We laughingly compiled a list the Navy would owe us as subjects of their "official project", i.e., missed meals, per diem, housing, etc. This had really turned out to be one hell of a day!

The Coast Guard pilot asked me to activate the beacon function of our radio in order to "home" in on the steady signal. Because the radio was "line of sight", and the C-130 was flying at 10,000 feet, we supposed that we were probably no more than a hundred miles apart. Thereupon, it wasn't more than 20 minutes before we could hear the distinct sound of the C-130 turbo-prop engines. The weather was beautiful, clear, with a few scattered clouds. I pulled out an orange flare, and told the pilot that we could hear him, and were about to light a flare.

"Tally Ho!" came the voice over the radio. "We have you dead ahead," the pilot called.

"Roger that." I replied." We have you in sight."

Charlie got out the camera, and we took a picture of the C-130 overhead. It was great to see him. We knew he was out of Barbers Point Naval Air Station, and it just made Hawaii seem that much closer.

I asked the pilot to give us a position so I could compare it with my plotted position. He had us off the Koko Head Vortac on the 037 radial at 127 miles. My calculations were 030 degrees from Kaneohe Bay between 120 and 130 miles. We were not more than 10 to 15 miles from my estimated position for our 55th day at sea.

The C-130 circled as we talked of what was to take place in the next few hours. The pilot told us that the Coast Guard would send a helicopter out to pick us up. This is where Charlie and I had some problems with their planning.

We had a gut feeling that if we were to allow the Coast Guard to come out and pick us up, we'd find ourselves in the morning papers as, "rescued." We didn't want that label, because this clearly wasn't a rescue effort. We were doing fine, had lots of fish, and knew we could make our own landfall in a few days. I asked the pilot about the disposition of our boat if a helicopter picked us up. He said that unfortunately they would have to sink it because it would be a hazard to navigation if left to drift around.

This didn't sit well with Charlie and me. In retrospect, it seems silly to have attached so much importance to *Courageous*, but leaving her out in the ocean to be sunk didn't seem the way to treat a raft that had carried us so far so faithfully. In fact, to this very day, I have kept *Courageous* through many many moves. We advised the Coast Guard that we did not want to leave our boat, and that we would continue on to sail to Hawaii.

In the meantime, the pilot was not only talking with us, he was relaying this information to the Coast Guard Search and Rescue people in Honolulu. He came back on the air, and explained that the Navy wanted us picked up, doctors were waiting for us. If we elected to continue our sail, the Navy would no longer complete its medical research, and would send the doctors back to California.

Charlie and I had a real dilemma on our hands. We recounted the doctors' concern that we would or could suffer permanent kidney damage on our trip. Our urine had become very dark and thick, but we had no problem passing it, and we were suffering no lower back pains. Would five days make or break us? We had to make some decisions straight away. We had an overwhelming desire to make our own landfall. But then neither of us had health insurance, and if we were indeed suffering some permanent physical damage we couldn't afford the medical costs. I was married, and if I were indeed suffering some permanent damage, I would be penalizing Judi by using all our money to keep me well. If we were an official Navy project, the Navy would take care of our medical needs.

Considering our hopes to start a survival equipment store and sell our kit, our initial decision was to make our own landfall. Anyway I had from the start carried a vision of stepping off *Courageous* on a beautiful beach in Hawaii.

However, if we elected to continue to Hawaii, and the Navy neglected to complete the medical research, then all the work in Oakland and all the things we had accomplished on the trip would be for nothing. The medical research was important not only to us, but could help save lives in the future. I hated to forfeit that part of our trip.

While Charlie and I discussed all our options, the Coast Guard pilot came on the line to tell us that a Coast Guard cutter would be in our area the next day, and they had agreed to pick us up along with the boat.

It was plain to see that the Coast Guard appreciated our feeling, and were trying to work with us. We finally made an agreement with them. We would agree to be picked up so long as the Coast Guard didn't use the term, "rescue." Next, they had to pick up *Courageous*. The entire conversation took place over almost a two-hour period while the C-130 circled overhead. It was all agreed to, and the pilot advised that the cutter would be out early the next morning for the pickup. He asked us to stay as close as possible to our present position which led us to deploy the sea anchor, and prepare to take down the sail.

After we reached an understanding with the C-130 pilot, he advised that the cutter should be in the area for pickup at about 0800 hours the next morning. The C-130 pilot said that he too would be out early the next morning to help coordinate the effort. He signed off, and headed back to Honolulu.

The mood on *Courageous* was one of relief, and some discouragement. We were relieved that we were soon going to be in Hawaii to receive professional medical help, and discouraged that we had sailed 2700 miles only to be denied our own land fall less than 150 miles from our destination. Although the Navy considered the expedition a success, they had not made the arduous 2700 mile trip. We understood their not wanting to pay doctors to wait in Hawaii for a week or more until we made landfall, but we didn't understand why they sent the doctors before the 60 days were up or until they had heard from us.

Nevertheless, we made our decision, and looked forward to rejoining civilization, and oh yes, having pancakes. We celebrated by drinking almost all our reserve water, and toasted each other for being strong, and not giving up the first week. From then on we just sat back and relaxed. I looked around the raft, the sky, and the ocean, trying to imprint on my memory the total environment. We had become so accustomed to being in the raft, I suspected we might forget how beautiful it was on the open sea. On the other hand, I was tired of being wet and cold, and looked forward to a dry bed.

We had lost so much weight that it was difficult to sleep in the same position for any length of time before our bones felt as if they were pushing right through the skin. We simply had lost all our fat padding. However, continually surprising was how overall good we felt. Neither of us had had even so much as a sniffle. We only had the salt water sores from the day of our nightmarish upset. Other than that, our clothing had worked well in not only keeping us warm, but in preventing chafing against the raft.

It was hard to comprehend that we had only one more night on *Courageous*. The finale had come up so swiftly that it took awhile for it all to sink in. Charlie and I talked about different aspects of the trip, and what we would do in Hawaii. I was anxious to see Judi, but wasn't sure if she could come to Hawaii. The Coast Guard was going to notify her that we were going to be picked up, and she would call Nancy.

We had no money with us, so we were a little apprehensive about arriving in Hawaii with no way to buy food, clothing, or a motel room. I hoped to phone Judi collect so she could wire me money.

Since we were subjects of an official Navy project, we hoped to check into the BOQ (Bachelor Officer Quarters), stay there, and eat in the galley. We might even have to go directly to the hospital for awhile to complete the medical research. After that, we had no firm plans. We laughed to recall how we had expected to land on a deserted Hawaiian beach, and sleep under *Courageous* the first night. We had an abundance of dried fish so we wouldn't have starved. Excuse the pun.

That last night was a beautiful one. The seas were a "Force 4" with long swells and a steady breeze and stars as bright as they had been on any night of the trip. And were we tired! With the sail down and the sea anchor out, we decided to rest as much as possible because tomorrow was going to be a busy day. With pick-up scheduled for 0800 hours the next day, we needed time in the morning to arrange and organize the boat. Thereon, we slept well, although we didn't sleep very long this last night.

The next morning we were up at daybreak, and began to organize the boat. I unpacked the flares so we'd have them available in case we would need them to help the Coast Guard cutter locate us. And we made sure that we had the radios out and ready to use. We expected the Coast Guard C-130 to be out early so we would be ready to talk to him.

We deflated and packed the solar stills, took down the mast, folded and packed the sail and lines. Leaving aside the flares and a compass, we repacked the survival kit. We tried cleaning our clothes as much as we could so we wouldn't stink too badly. Having become so accustomed to the smell, we weren't sure if we smelled or not, but since we'd been slopping around in sea water, dead fish, blood and birds in the same clothes for two months, there wasn't much doubt about it.

By 8 o'clock on the morning of August 28th, we had everything in order for pickup, but saw no cutter nor heard an aircraft call. I go into detail about this last day because of the importance in demonstrating the difficulties in locating someone in the open ocean, and why it is important that a sailor be self-sufficient in his ability to survive and save himself. It is not my intention to downgrade the Coast Guard here, because of the time 13 years later that they saved my life after I ditched the aircraft six hundred miles south of Hawaii. But lest the uninitiated believe there is a safety blanket covering the oceans in the form of a Coast Guard, or any other organization, military or civilian, I would advise them to take this part of the book to heart.

At almost 10 o'clock in the morning we got a call from the C-130 pilot advising that the cutter was having difficulty and that he was setting out to locate the cutter. After a half hour or more, the C-130 called again to say he was running low on fuel and would have to return to Barbers Point to refuel. We never did know if he had located the cutter, but there was nothing we could do but wait. It was a clear day, and we were getting sunburned for we no longer had the tarp to shade us. In fact, this was the only day we got sunburned on the entire trip.

Just after noon we heard a motor. It was a dull sound, more like a diesel engine. We kept our eyes glued to the horizon in the direction of the sound, and finally saw black smoke out there. I stood up to get more range with the radio, and called what I hoped was the cutter. There was no answer. We theorized that we were still out of range, or that the cutter was not monitoring the emergency frequency.

We watched the smoke as it became darker and darker, and finally saw the white hull of a ship. There was no doubt that it had to be the cutter because not many ships besides Coast Guard vessels have white hulls. The smoke and hull became larger and larger. They weren't more than four or five miles away. Again I tried the radio, but got some garbled noise that we couldn't understand. Then I broadcast in the blind that we were going to fire some flares, and light some orange smoke. Charlie and I drew up the last bits of our energy and shot flares, and flashed signal mirrors.

The cutter made a turn, and began to steam around the horizon in a large circle away from us! Mind you, this was a ship looking for us as castaways. Eventually it stopped, and they set off a huge orange smoke bomb.

Charlie and I were dumbfounded! I said, "What the hell are we suppose to do, sail over to them?" It was 2 o'clock in the afternoon, and they were still looking! The cutter started up again, and looked as though he was coming directly to us. I again got on the radio, and broadcast in the blind. The response was as garbled as the first time, but the signal was stronger. I held the compass, and took a bearing on the cutter. By adding 180 degrees I figured the reciprocal, or the cutter's heading to us, and I broadcast the cutter's heading to us in the blind.

"Coast Guard Cutter, this is *Courageous*. We have you in sight, steer a course of 290 degrees, steer 290 degrees to *Courageous*. *Courageous* is dead ahead! *Courageous* is dead ahead! How do you hear over?"

Again I heard a garbled answer. Then, to our total disbelief, the cutter began a turn away from us! Again I got on the radio and repeated the heading to us. It was useless. I decided to hold any more calls for the time as I thought he might begin to realize the radios were "line of sight," so if he didn't hear us anymore he would realize that he was getting further away. The cutter's hull soon disappeared, then the smoke, and finally we no longer heard the muffled sound of the engine.

About an hour later, around three o'clock , we had another call from the C-130 pilot. He advised that he would try to locate the cutter, and give him a heading to us. Fifteen minutes later, another call came from the C-130 pilot telling us that he had climbed to a higher altitude in order to put both the cutter and us within his sight. He then helped direct the cutter from the air.

The Coast Guard cutter came along side at about five that evening. They threw us a line, we tied it off, and the crew pulled us to the cutter. A Jacob's ladder was thrown over the side, and we climbed aboard. I couldn't believe how weak I was in trying to climb that ladder. On deck we found neither of us could walk or stand on our own. If we held on to something we could remain upright, but walking was not easy. A TV person interviewed us while we sat on the deck. We were all smiles. After the interview, they asked in a polite way if we cared to take a shower. Later we learned that we just about bowled them over with an effusive odor!

We were led below deck into a stateroom where we undressed near a shower room. I couldn't stand so I just sat down on the shower drain, and had a great shower. The crew canvassed the smallest men aboard for clothing that would come closest to fitting us. Everything was away too big. No matter! It was great to have on clean clothes.

We were even more dehydrated now that we hadn't had a drink all day, so I drank some shower water. A sailor brought us Coca Colas, and it was like honey going down my throat. We had just finished the Cokes when word came down from the medics that we were not to eat or drink anything until we got to Tripler Army Hospital, where we would disembark. The Captain came to tell us that they stored *Courageous*, and that a helicopter with a doctor aboard would land on deck in a few minutes, look us over, and take us back to Honolulu.

With the chopper a few minutes away, we were led back up on deck to await its arrival. It came in and hovered over the stern of the cutter, but not landing since there was no landing platform. When the doctor was lowered to the deck in a basket, to our surprise, it was Dr. Peter Lee, the doctor who had done all the work for us in Oakland.

Peter asked us how we felt, and we told him, "fine." He asked us if we thought we could make it to the basket to be lifted into the chopper. We told him we felt just a little weak. The crew helped us to the basket, and we were lifted into the chopper. We were off to Honolulu!

It was a short flight, the island of Oahu rose out of the water like a green emerald. We flew over Pali Pass, and down the leeward side of the mountains into Honolulu International Airport. When we landed, there were many reporters, and we were allowed a short time for interviews before being led to a waiting ambulance. My thoughts still on food, I asked Dr. Lee if we could stop at a McDonalds before we got to the hospital because it was almost six thirty, and the Army mess would be closed. I hated the thought of lying there in the hospital, and not be able to eat until morning. Everyone laughed, but I was serious.

When we arrived at the hospital, we were taken for our physicals first. On the more solid floor of the hospital we were able to walk for the doctors, and they had us walk as straight a line as possible. They drew a couple of vials of blood from each of us, but as soon as they took our blood pressure they discontinued the blood draws. They obtained the same low readings of blood pressure that we had on the boat: sixty over zero. We were willing to have more blood drawn, but the doctors thought it might be dangerous. When all the tests were finished, we reached the important stuff, i.e., food! Dr. Lee asked us what we had eaten in the last 24 hours, and we told him raw fish, and most recently, a Coke. He thought if we could eat raw fish, we could probably keep down anything the Army might serve us. Indeed the mess was closed, but a nurse went in and gathered whatever she could find. She brought back a couple of salami sandwiches, two quarts of half-and-half milk, four cans of some kind of chocolate milk drink, and some cookies. Well, normally I don't like salami sandwiches, but I ate that sandwich, then drank the whole quart of half-and-half, two cans of chocolate milk, and ate some cookies. Amazingly I held it all down.

At our first weigh-in I had dropped from 185 to 128 pounds. Charlie had dropped from 180 to 132. We looked like returnees from a prisoner of war camp. It was a miracle that we looked so bad but felt so well.

Tests finished, I got to crawl into a nice warm, dry hospital bed. It was heaven, but I didn't sleep all that well, primarily because I was so uncomfortable from eating so much food.

The next morning we ordered our pancakes, and once again over-ate. We each had the first bowel movement in over a month. We hadn't absorbed much of the food we had just eaten because our intestines had dried out so badly. It was a little embarrassing to save our stool to be analyzed, but the Navy made certain they got their money's worth out of us.

Our hospital stay lasted two days. To my astonishment, the dentist discovered, or rather, did not discover, a cavity that a dentist found in my teeth a month prior to the trip. We had brushed our teeth with sea water the entire trip, and VOILA! my tooth decay was gone. To this day I think that there is something restorative in brushing with sea water. Even the dentist in Oakland who found the original cavity could not find it when I returned home.

Of course we had minor physical problems after the trip, the major one being that of eating and drinking as much as we could hold. Our bodies reacted as if we were still at sea, especially in the retention of water and making our feet swell. The latter cleared up after a couple of weeks.

We ate about 7000 calories a day for over a week, and didn't have trouble holding it down, although we may not have been absorbing much of it. It took about as long to gain the weight back as it did to lose it since I was back up to 185 in two months.

I had often kidded Charlie that he would become so horny on the trip he would marry the first girl he saw on the beach. Well, he didn't marry the first girl, but he and Nancy were married in Hawaii the following week.

We received hundreds of letters from all over the world congratulating us our success. It was fun to receive all the letters and inquiries about our survival kit. With this encouragement I was ready to get back to Oakland to start making them up and selling them.

Judi and Nancy flew in the day after we arrived. I think Judi was a little surprised to see how I looked. She had never seen me with a beard, long hair, and very skinny. We were really glad to see the girls, but as I said before, our sex drive had zeroed out and we just couldn't rise to the occasion for any kind of sex. I couldn't seem to get in a mental state to have sex. I guess it was a little disappointing to the ladies, and they probably suffered some feelings of rejection, but there just was no sex drive within us.

We completed all the tests at the hospital on the third day, and were released to our ladies. Royal Hawaiian Tours had contacted us, and gave us a package deal for hotel rooms, tours, shows, and rental cars all free of charge. In return for all the gracious gifts, we did a little promotion thing for them.

Charlie and I still had a tough time walking, not because of balance, but our feet were so swelled from the retention of water that it hurt to walk. We tried to keep them up as much as possible, but it was hard staying off our feet when we had so many free things to take advantage of.

We made a special trip out to Barbers Point Naval Air Station to thank the pilot who found us and acted as intermediary between us and his boss at the Coast Guard. We also went to the pier where the Coast Guard cutter was docked. We thanked them again, and they gave us all our gear and *Courageous*.

A pilot from our Navy squadron had flown to Hawaii, and

we were happy to hear all the stories we had missed since leaving San Francisco. We expected to send *Courageous* back by ship, but our friends said that their bomb bay was empty so we put *Courageous* in their Navy A-3 bomb bay. Our raft was waiting for us in Alameda when we reached home.

After a week in Hawaii, Judi and I flew back to San Francisco. Charlie and Nancy stayed in Hawaii for a honeymoon. My sex drive began to return as we ate steadily. We continued our medical studies back home for another month to make sure we had no permanent damage, and to see how our bodies reacted in recovery.

The trip was over twenty-seven years ago as of this writing. Not much has changed insofar as ocean survival goes. We do have good emergency radio coverage for most areas of the ocean today, although there are still many "dead" areas for emergency radio contact. And, of course, radios can still fail. Reverse osmosis machines have replaced solar stills as a means of making a dependable amount of water each day.

One item still lacking is a dual purpose life raft made so that it can be anchored to the water if the castaway is able to transmit and receive a reply to his position report, but with the capability of being sailed if a castaway is faced with saving himself. Also, even though today an emergency radio may be heard from almost anywhere in the world, one has to remember that those radios can fail, and they are good for a limited amount of time as the battery will slowly discharge. I can tell you from experience that putting all your eggs in one basket and depending on just an emergency radio can be very discouraging when you find the radio does not work.

Survival in the open ocean is no easy task. I have been lucky, but it's my belief that one makes his own luck. There are still hundreds of people lost at sea every year. Some are able to survive their ordeals, and live to tell riveting stories about how they survived. I dared the trip in *Courageous* to prove and demonstrate the equipment one needs to plan a successful survival situation. If a sailor or aviator follows some simple rules laid out in this book, and makes certain he has the proper equipment, survival in the open ocean and self rescue is possible. If the radio beacons work, and a downed pilot or sailor is picked up quickly, that is super, but he must plan on saving himself before attempting an ocean voyage.

I produced hundreds of SIG II survival kits until I finally

ran out of solar stills. I was able to convince one raft company to modify its rafts so they could be rigged with a sail. Unfortunately, the company has since been sold, and I got out of the survival business. I had grateful customers who actually had to use the sailing life raft, and it saved their lives, along with the SIG II survival kit. It was very satisfying to me. I regret that I have been so long in writing this book, because I think if I had written it sooner, others may have been saved. It has been my dream that this book will inspire sailors and pilots to demand that raft companies produce a raft that can be sailed. If just one company produced one, I'm sure others would follow.

If a sailing life raft is not available, a sailor should consider a way of rigging a sail on a dinghy. I am not suggesting that a dinghy should be used as a life raft, but if a sailor is faced with his boat sinking, and has time to release both his life raft and dinghy, he will at least have the option of saving himself. With a round life raft, the castaway must depend on someone else to save his or her life. He will have forfeited the option of sailing to safety, and can only sit and drift where wind and waves take him.

As my favorite sailing buddy, Pat Royce says, "Happy Sailing", and I might add, happy flying. Life can be an adventure if you make it so.

Contents of Ocean Survival Kit

- Reverse Osmosis Pump (item substituted for Solar Distillation Kit)
- Hand Spear
- 12 Laminated Pilot Charts
- Laminated Solargram
- Survival Instruction Manual
- Advanced First Aid Manual
- 2 Pencils
- Small Items Bag
- Graduated Water Bag
- 35 sq.ft. Hi-Vis Orange Tarp
- 50' Nylon Line
- 2 Sponges
- 2 Day-Night Flares
- Signal Mirror
- 6.38 Cal. Signal Flares
- Pen Gun for Flares
- Zinc Oxide
- Raft Repair Clamps
- 4 ft. Plastic Tubing
- Flashlight plus 2 Alkaline Batteries, 1 spare bulb
- Logbook
- 100 yd. 90 lb. Fishing Line
- 1 Gal. Water Storage Bag
- Fishing Weights
- Knife Sharpening Hone
- Folding Gaff
- First Aid Kit – 7 Adhesive Bandages, Tweezers, 2" x 5 yd. Gauze, Betadine, 12 Tablets Dramamine, 1 oz. Methiolate, 24 Aspirin, Scissors, 1" x 5" Adhesive Tape, Pre-threaded Sutures
- Drinking Bottle
- Survival Knife
- Food & Vitamin Supplies – 15 packages Glucose Sugar, 6 packages of Multi-vitamins
- 6 small Fish Hooks
- 3 Large Fish Hooks 135 lb. Leader
- Plotter
- Liquid filled Compass
- Rubberized Nylon package to hold items and use for water storage